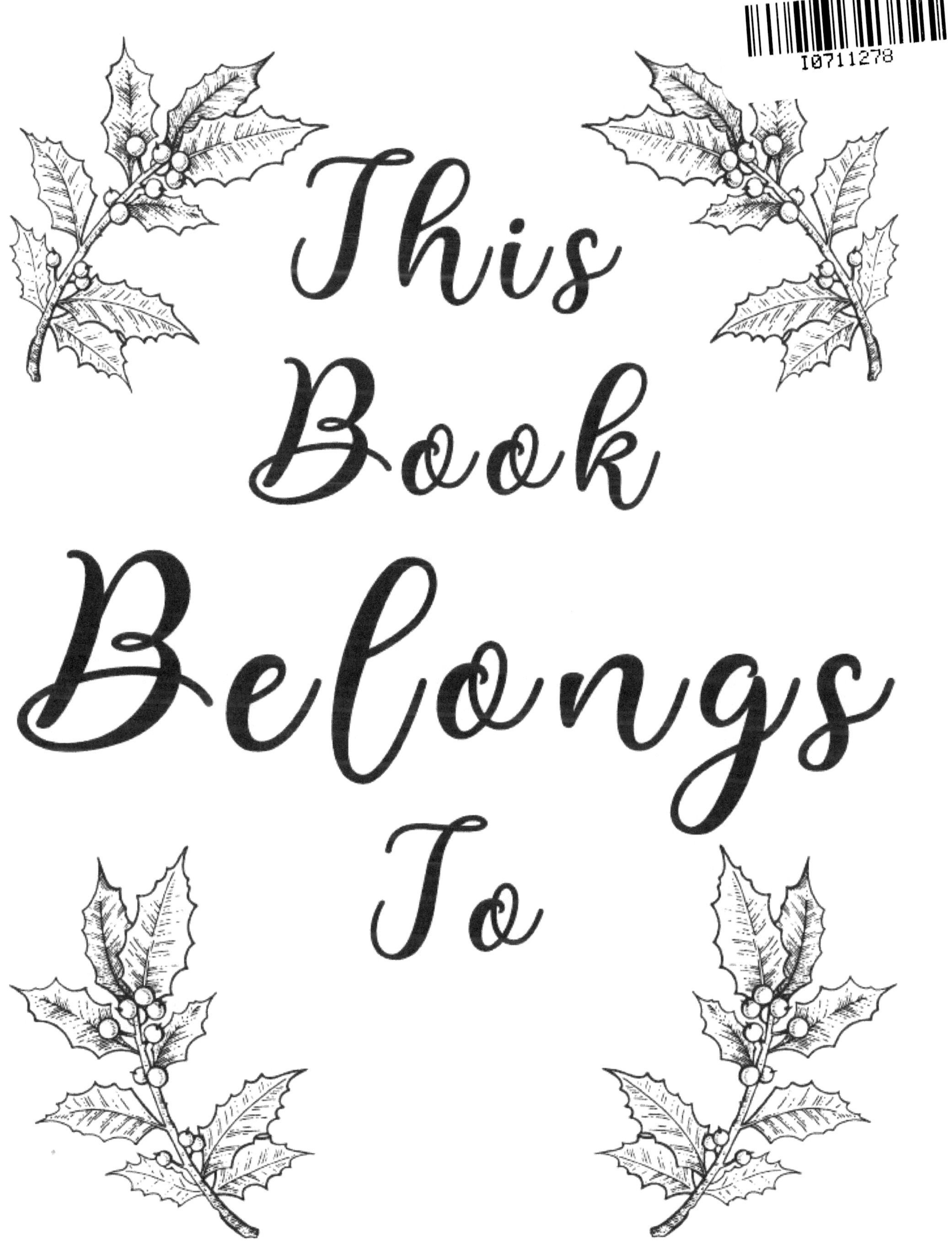
This
Book
Belongs
To

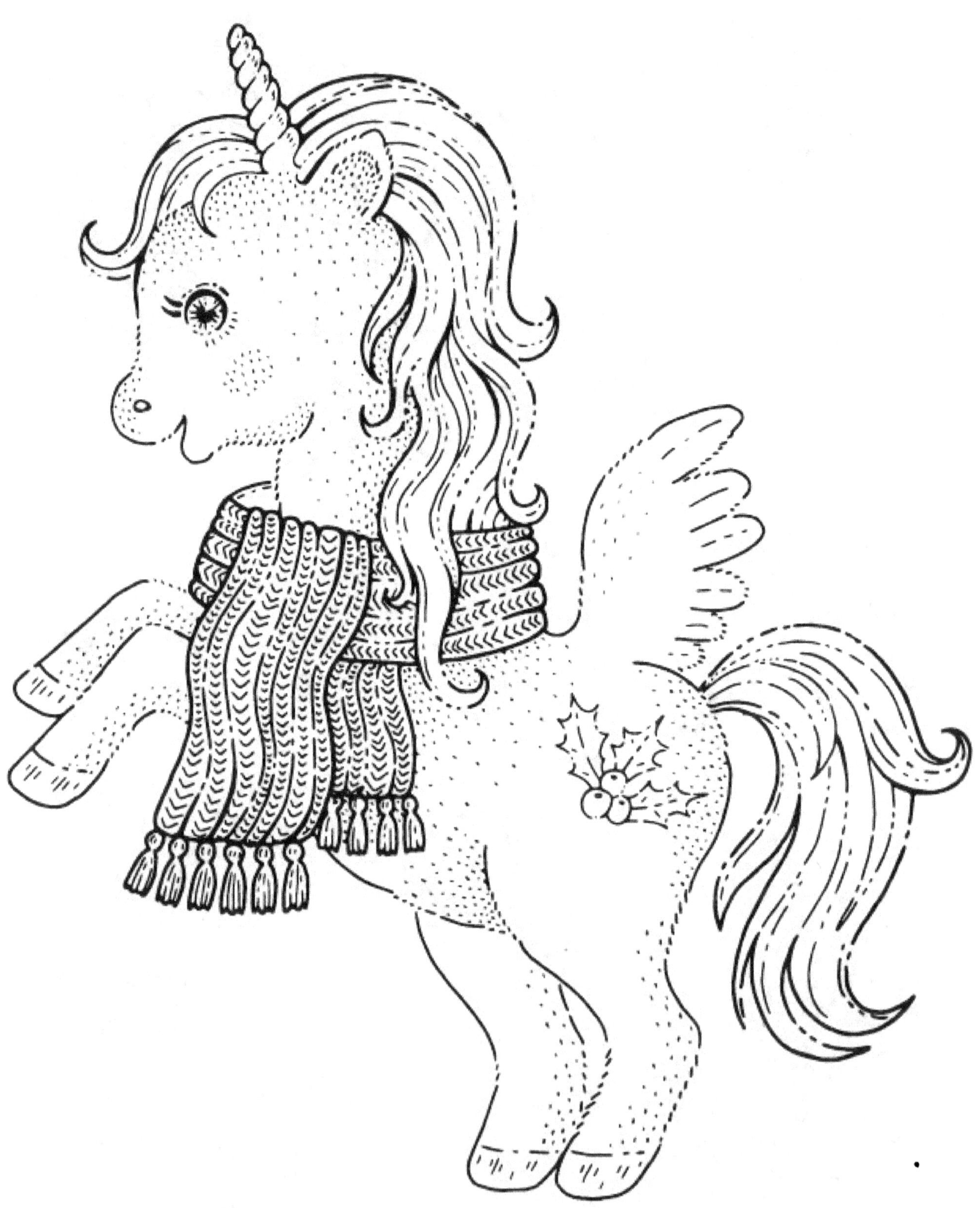

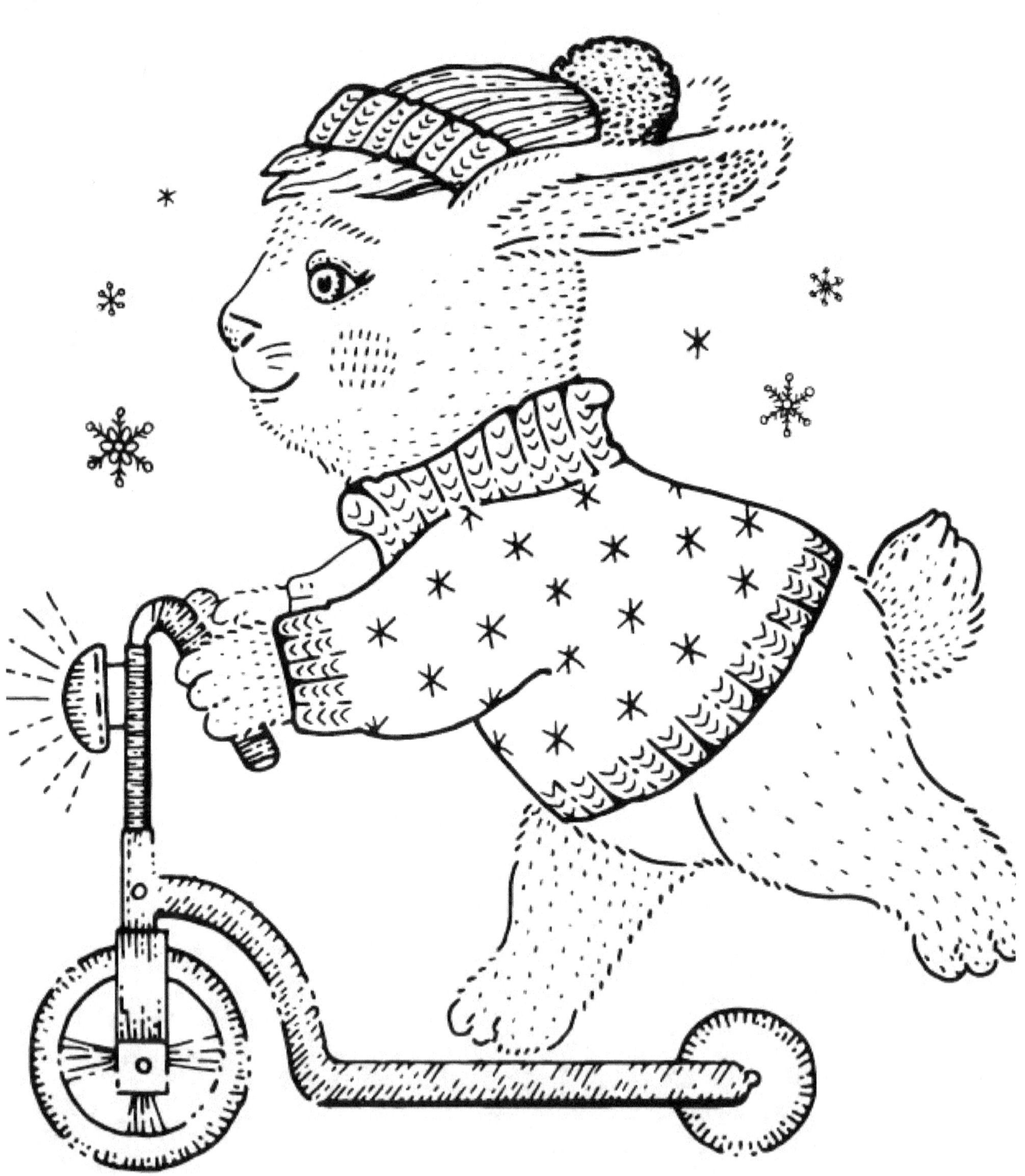

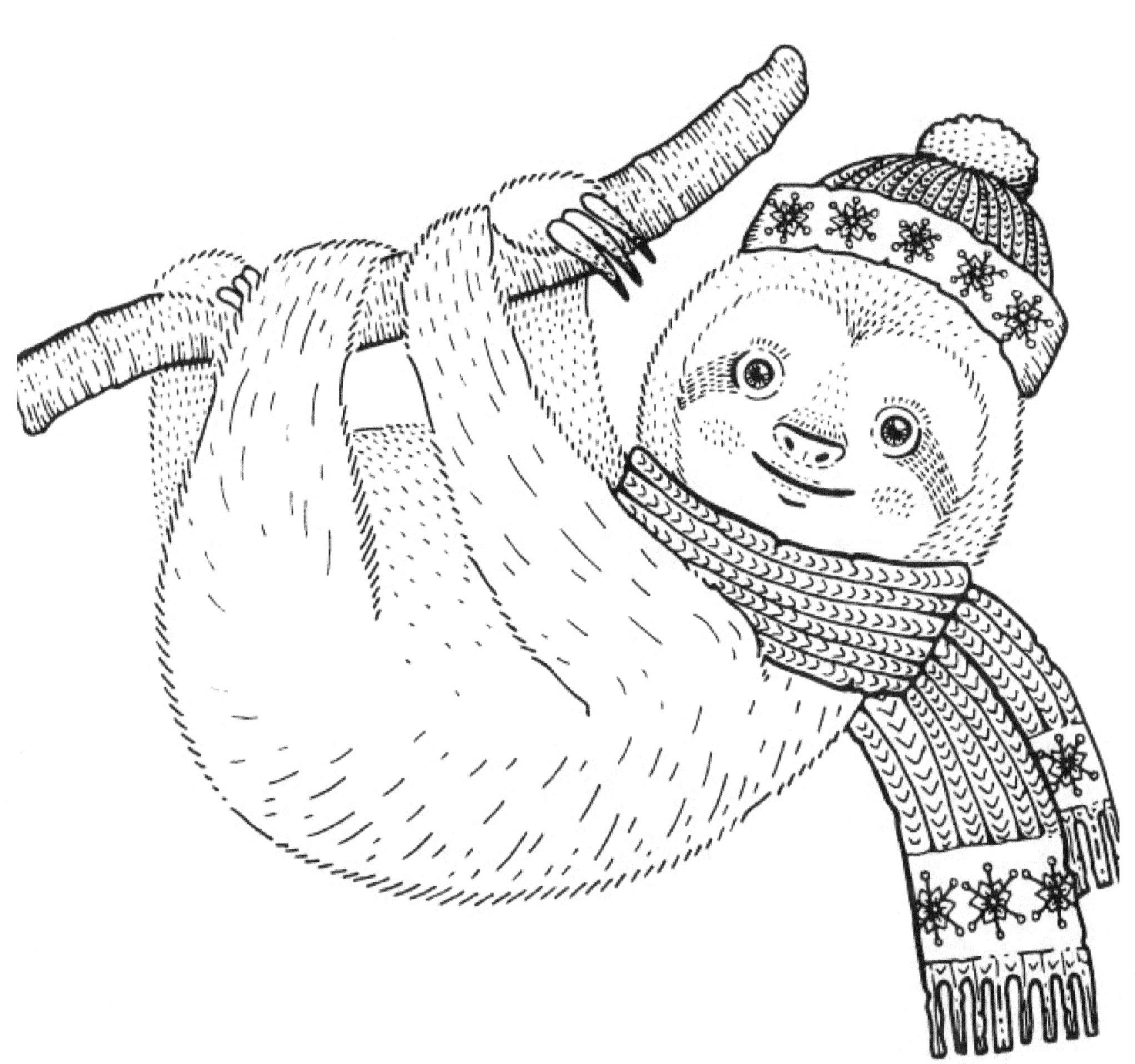

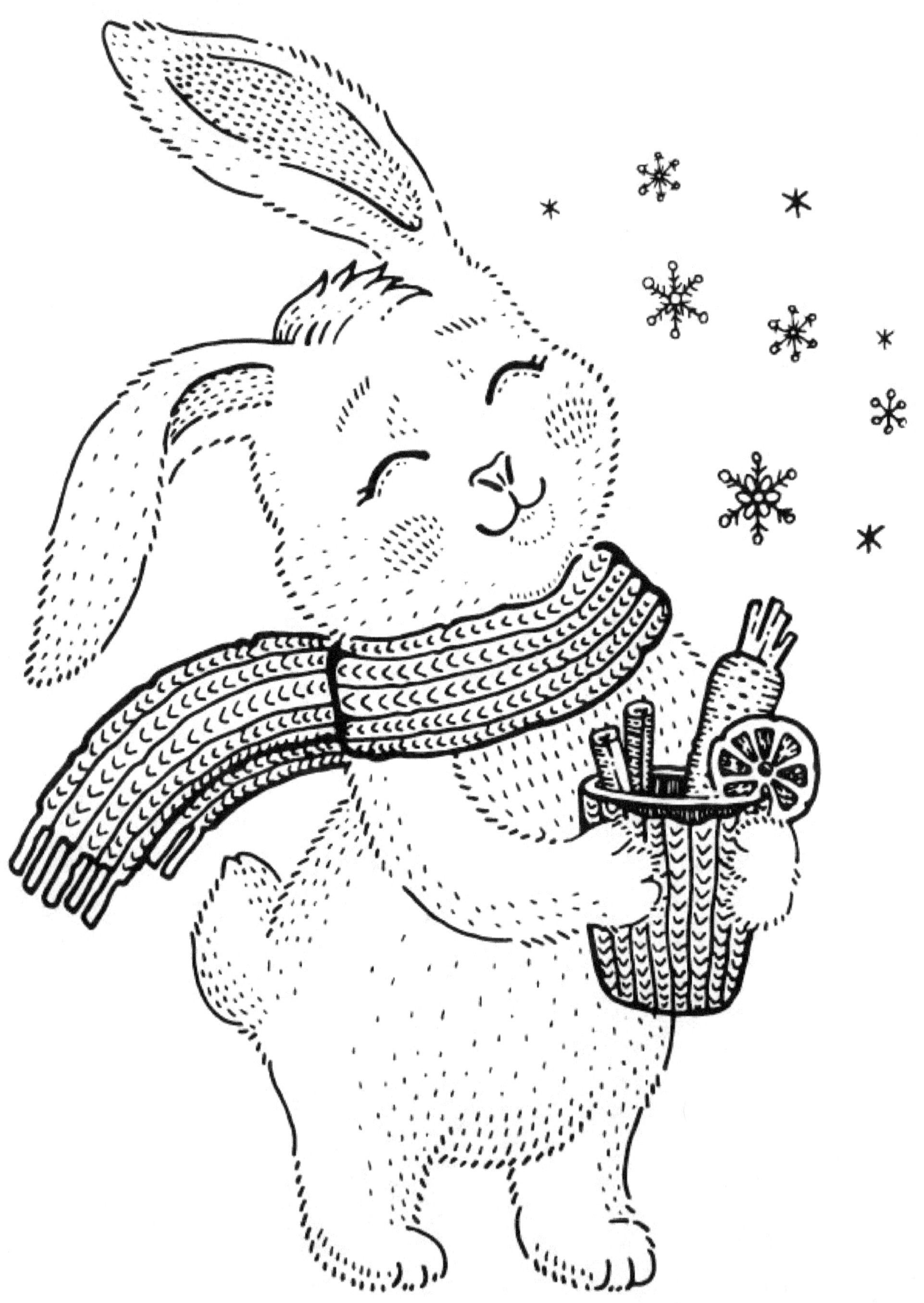

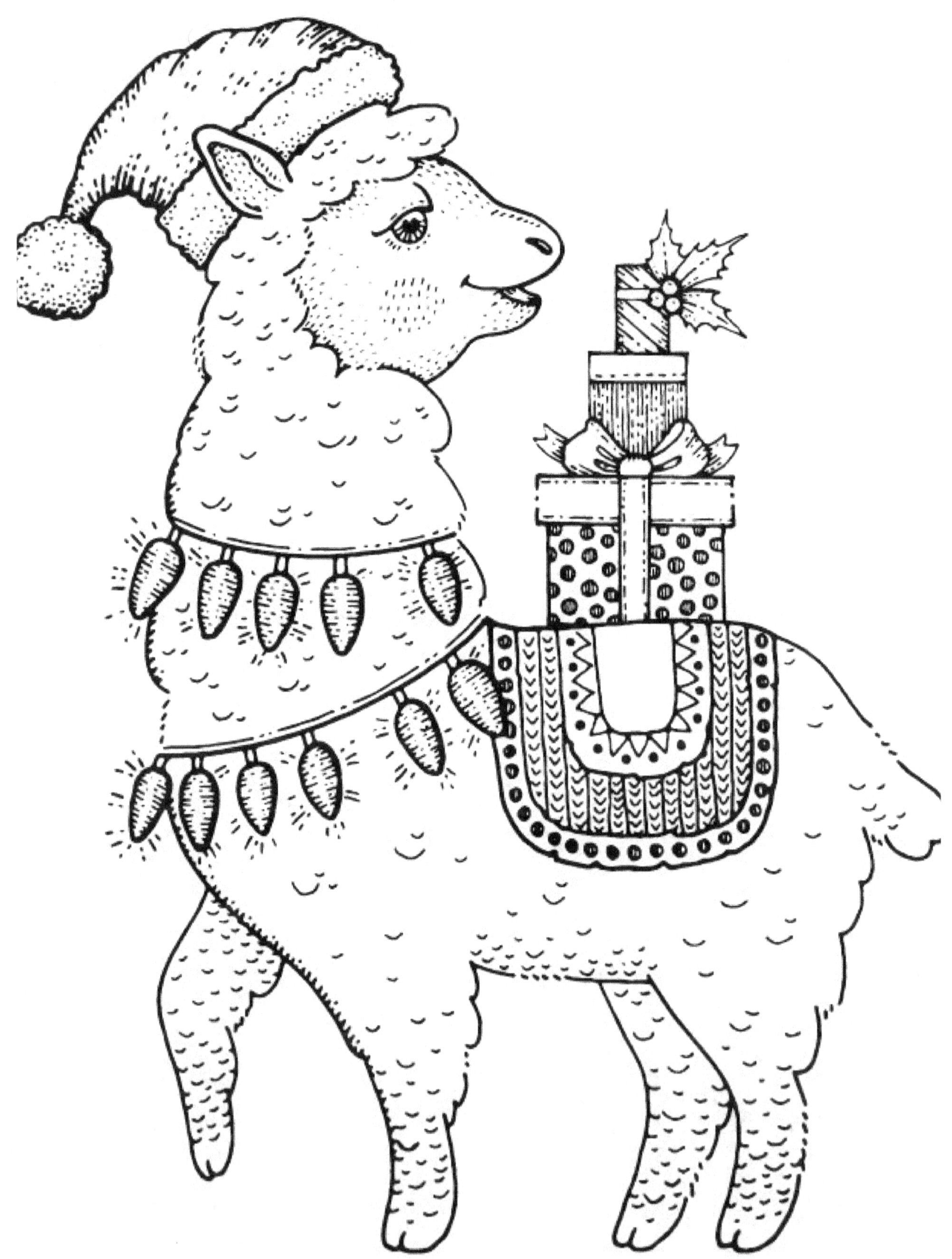

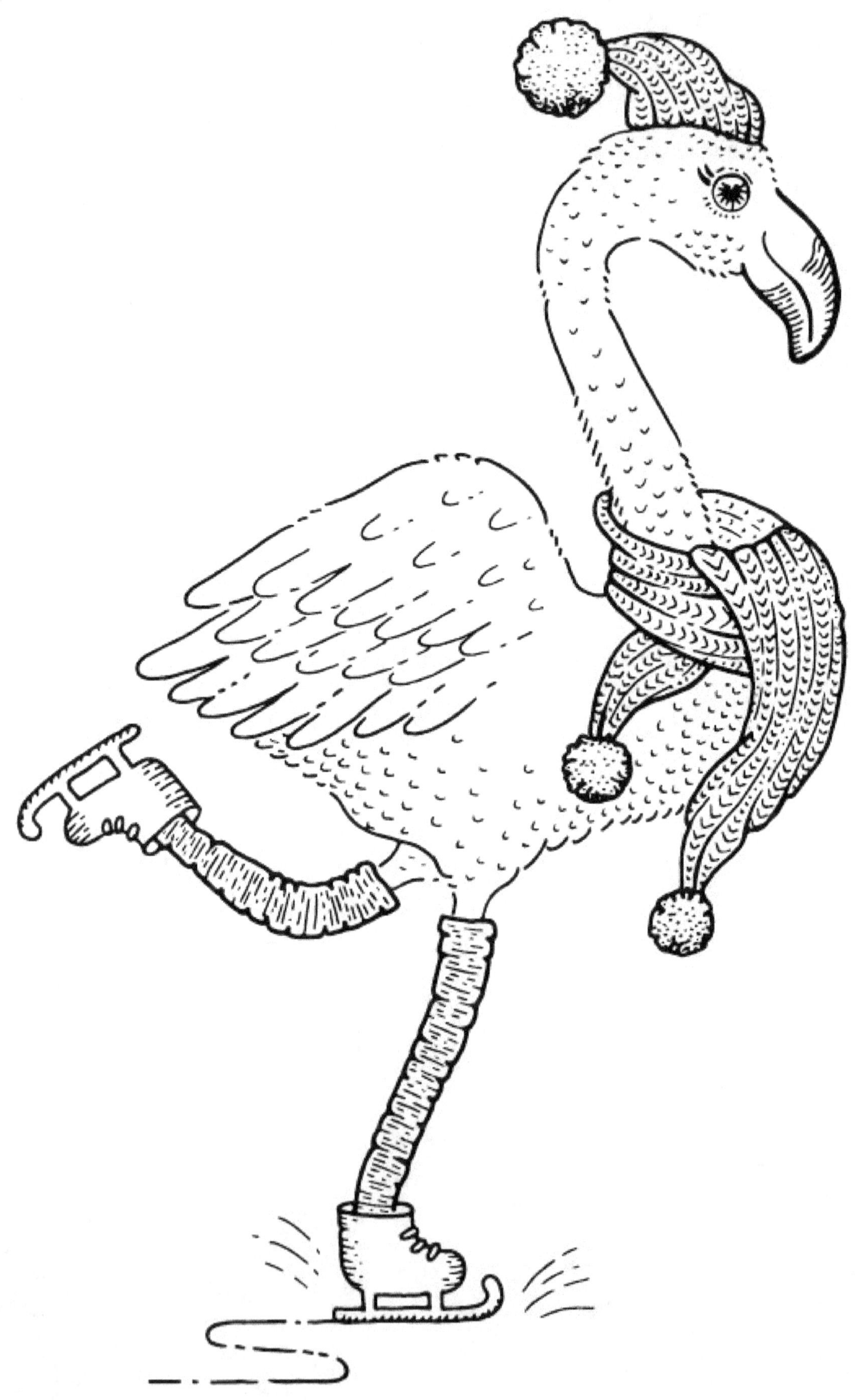

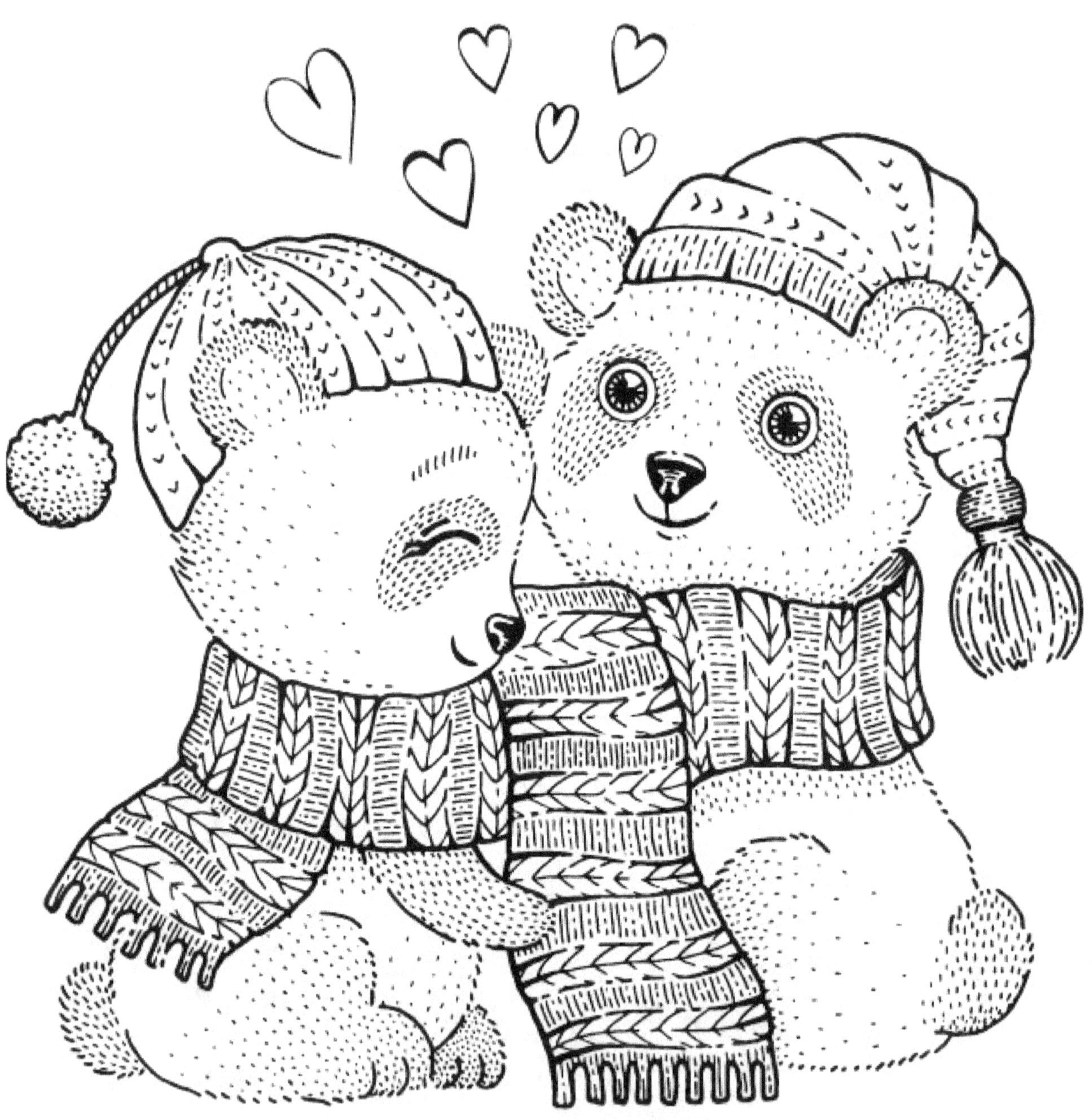

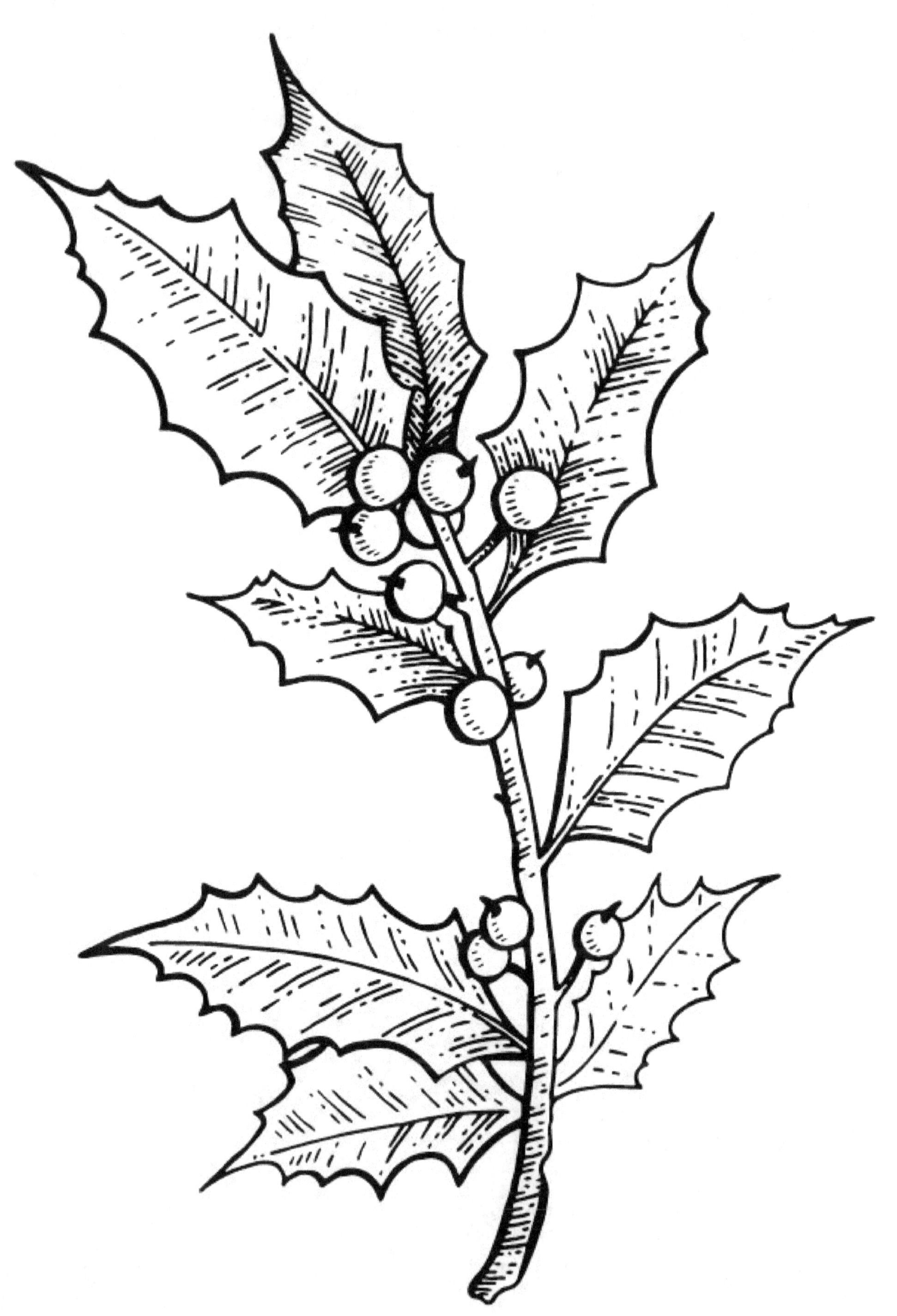

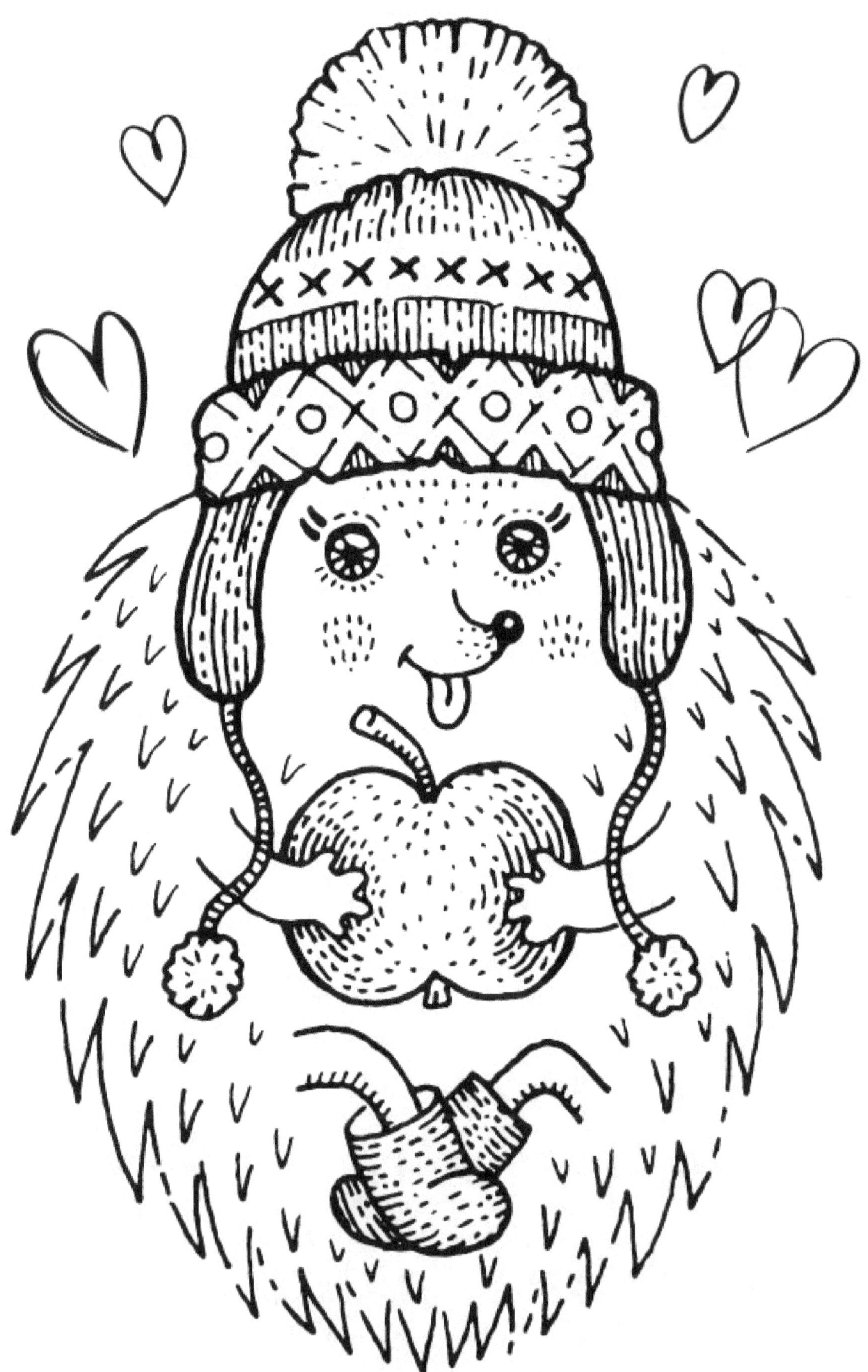

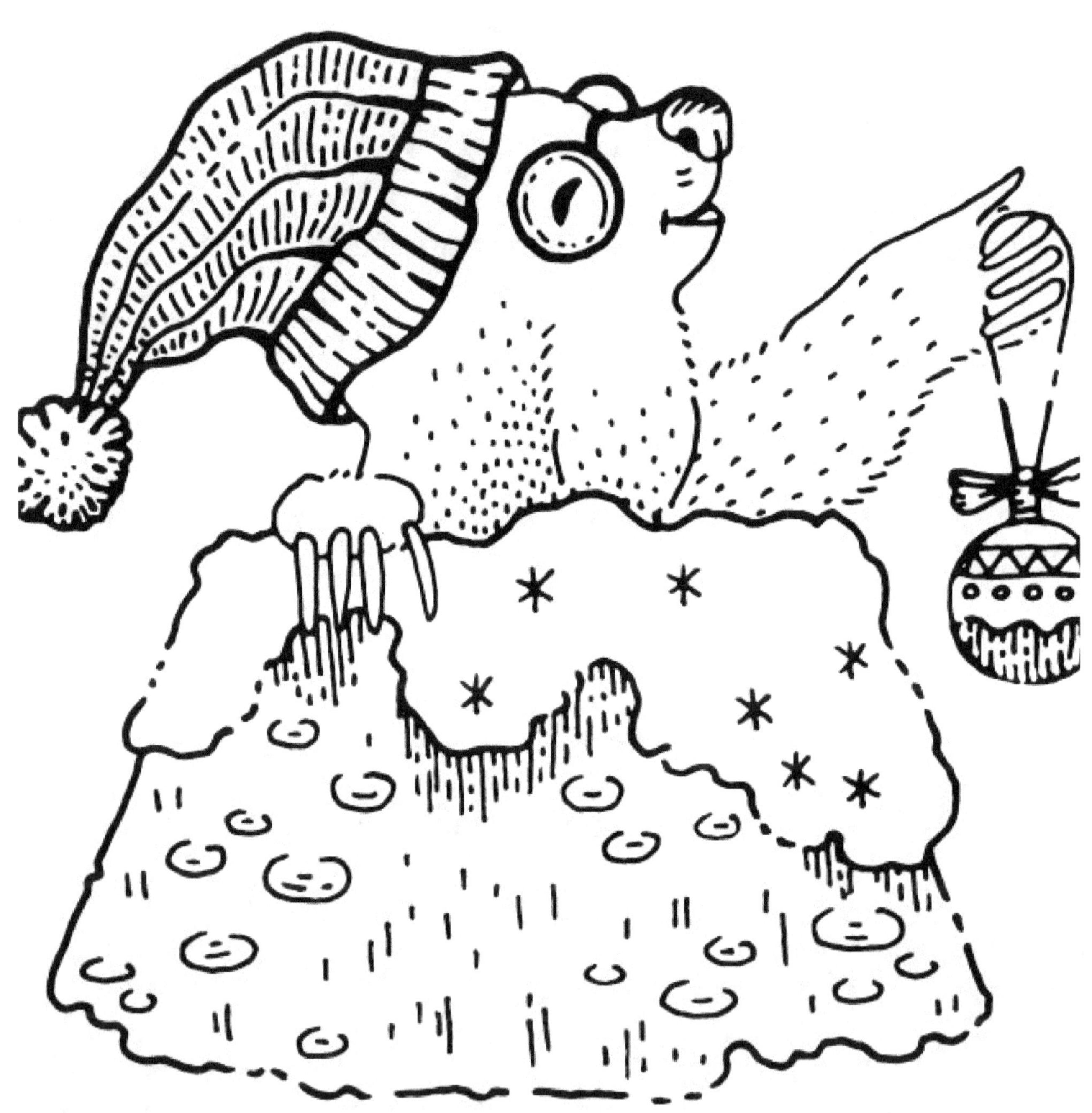

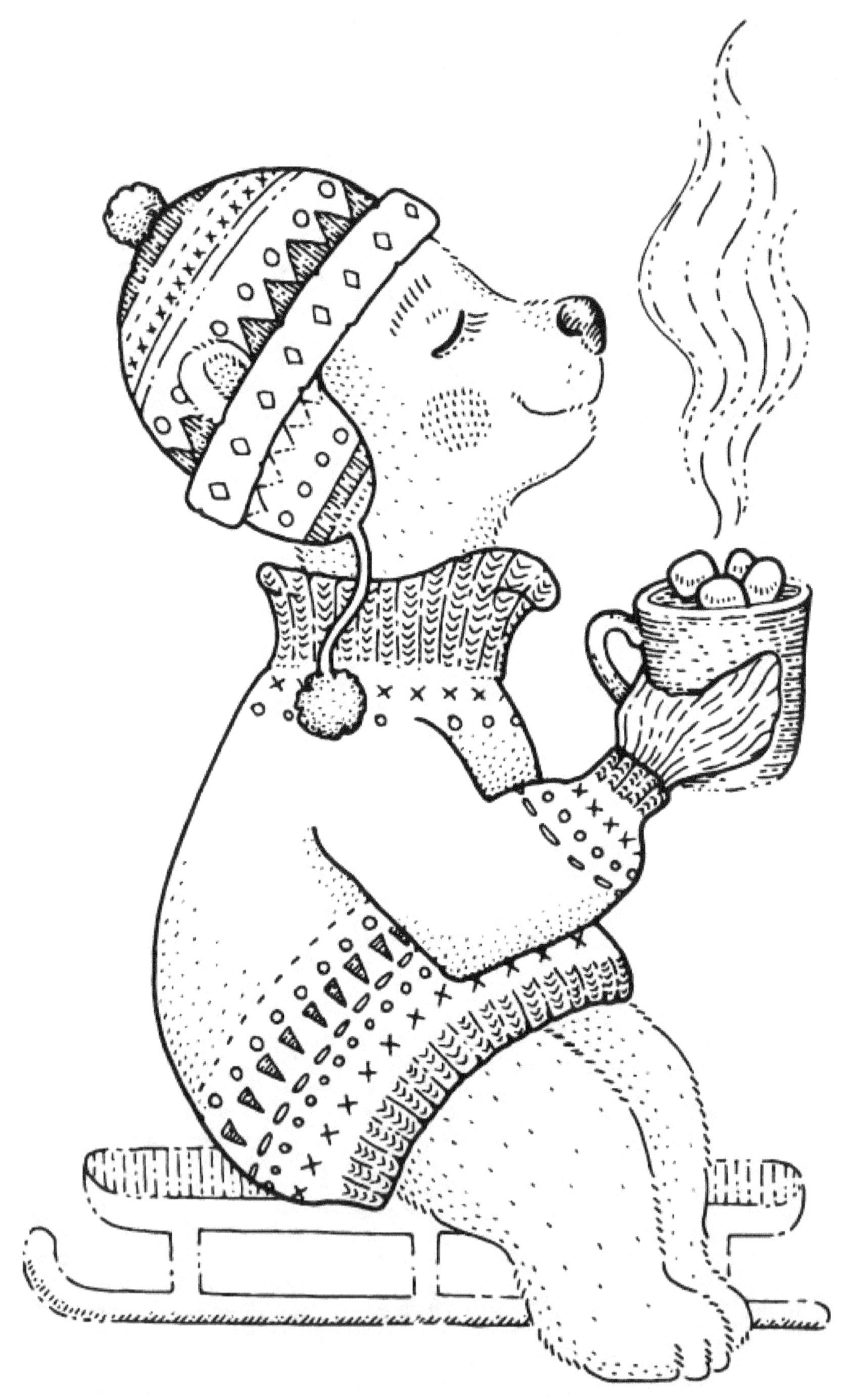

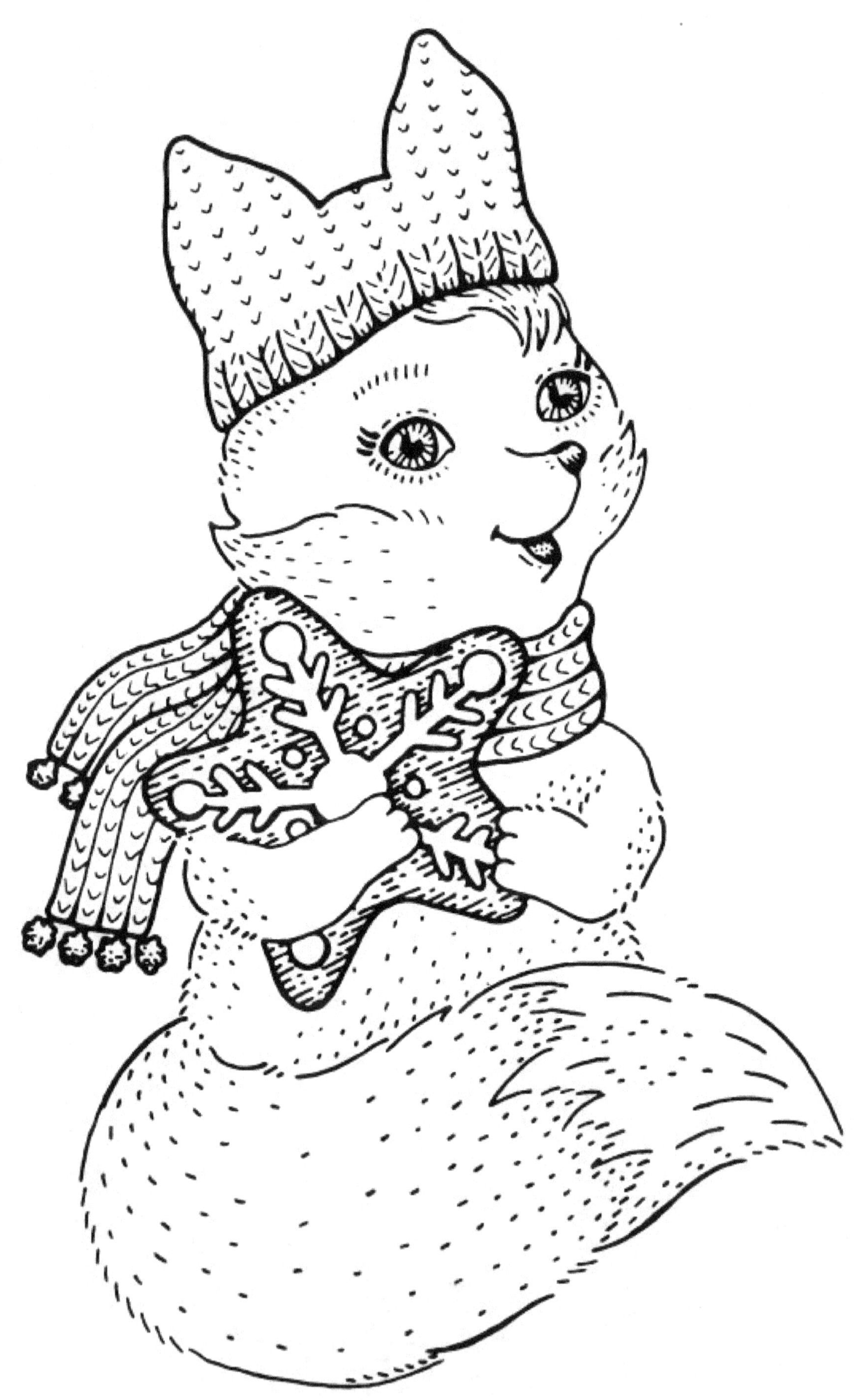

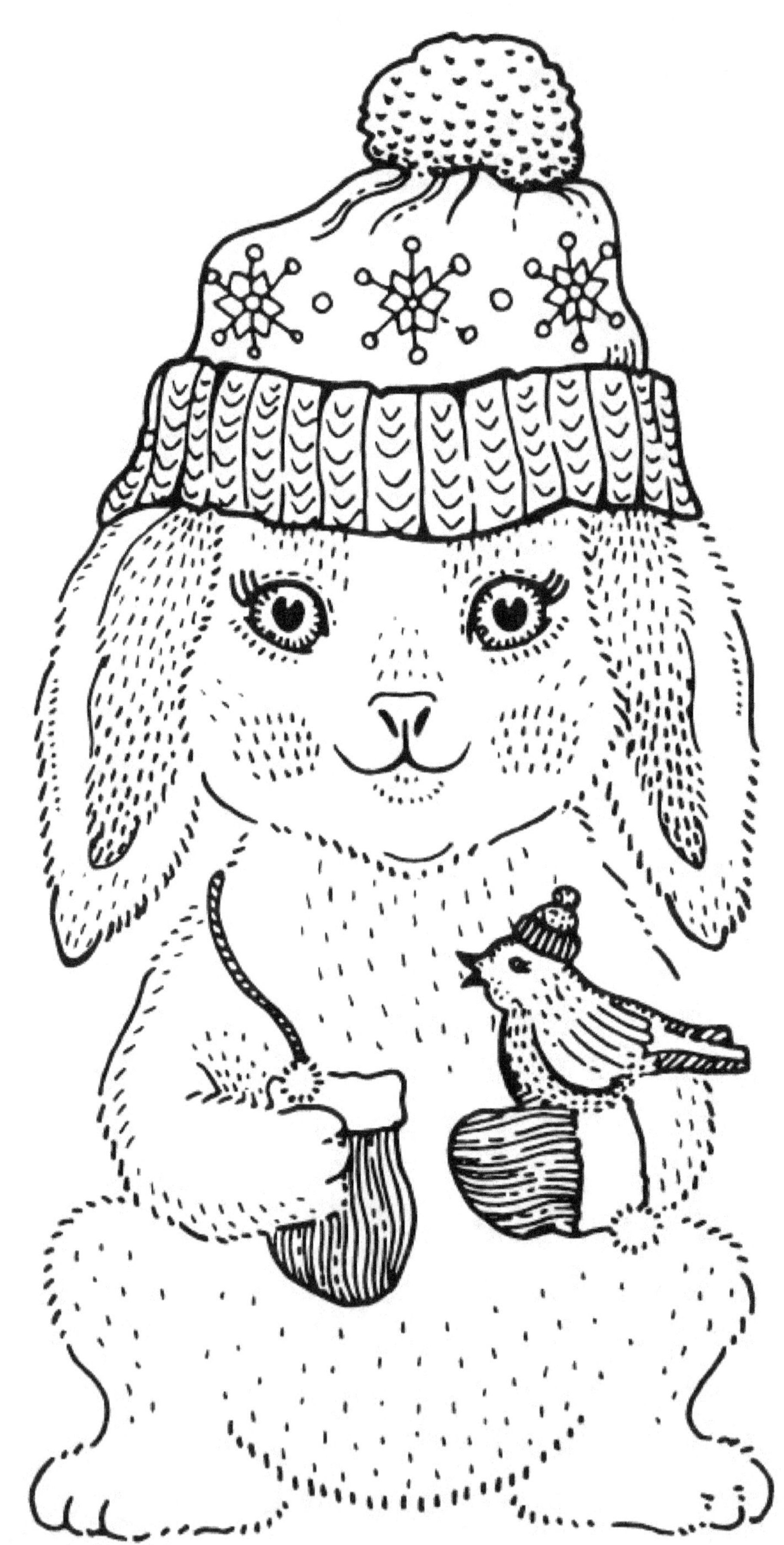

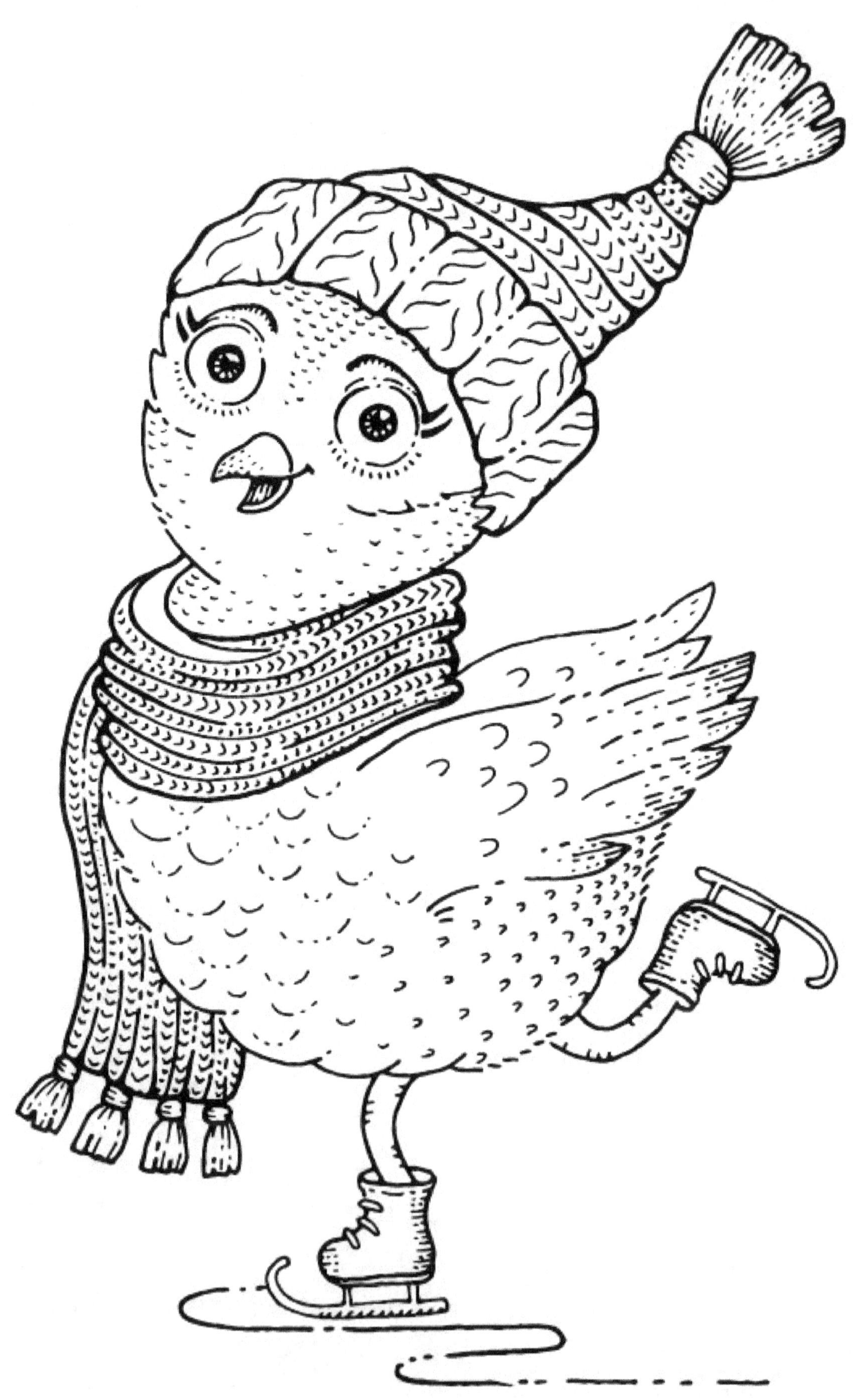

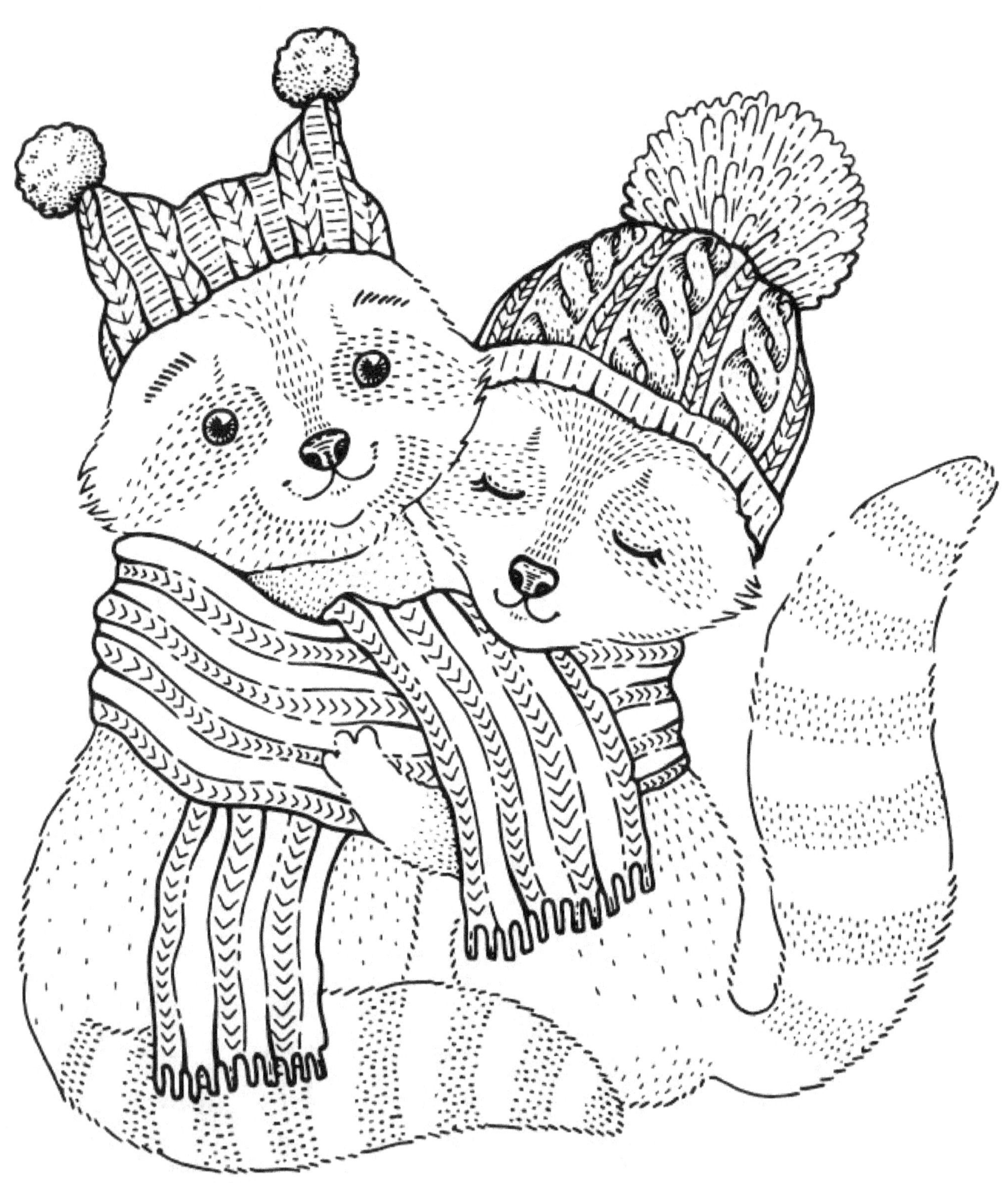

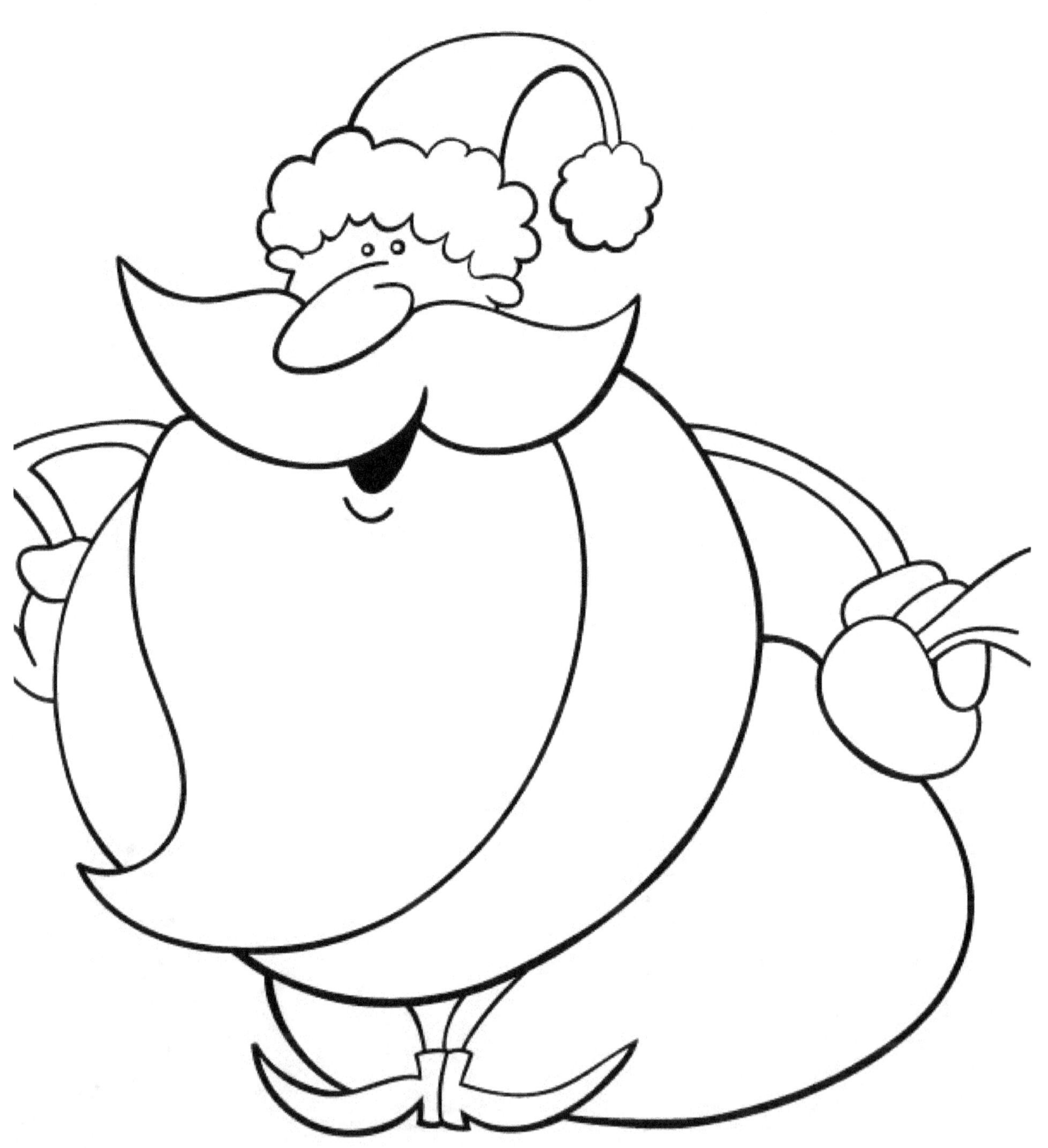

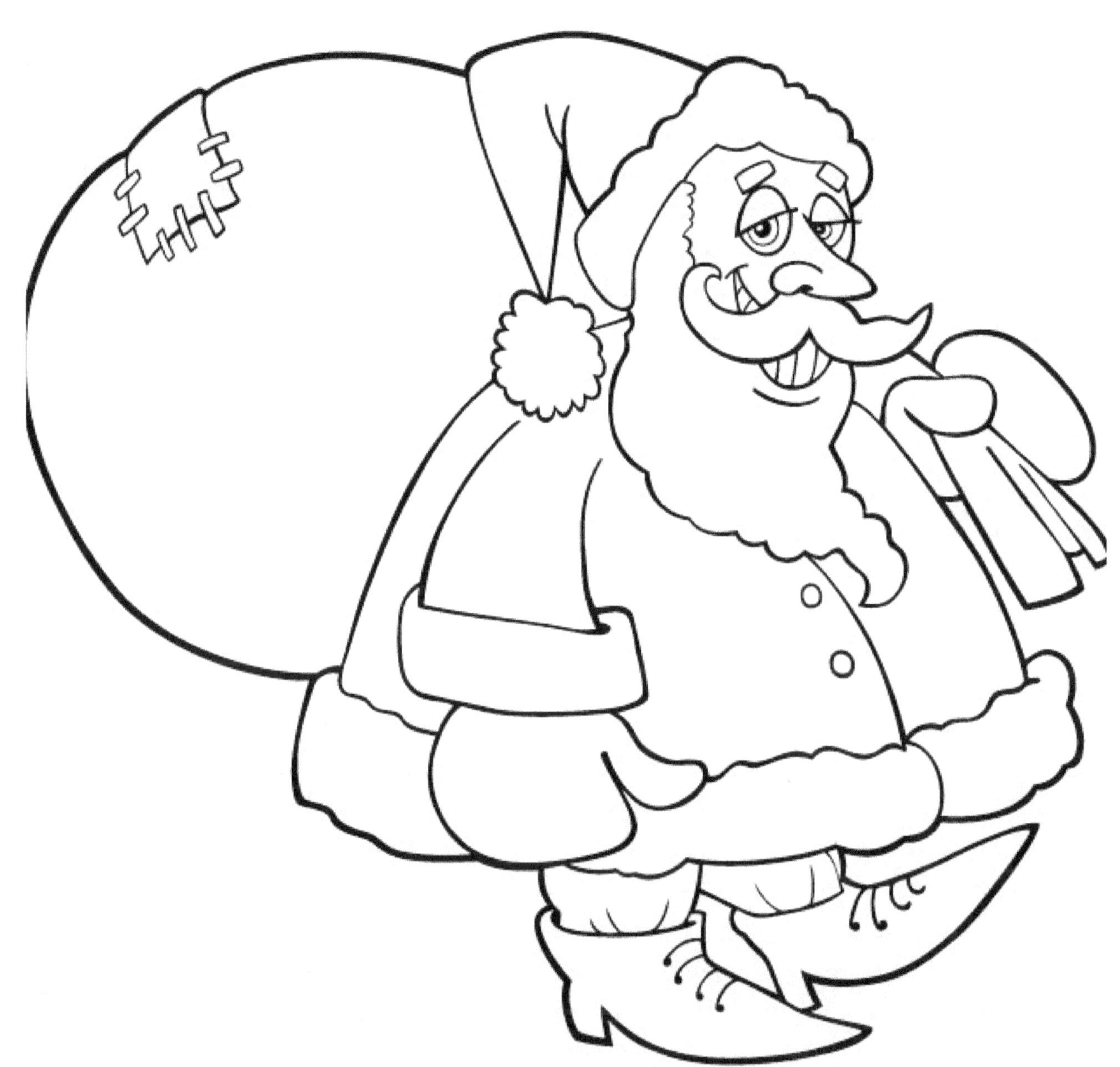

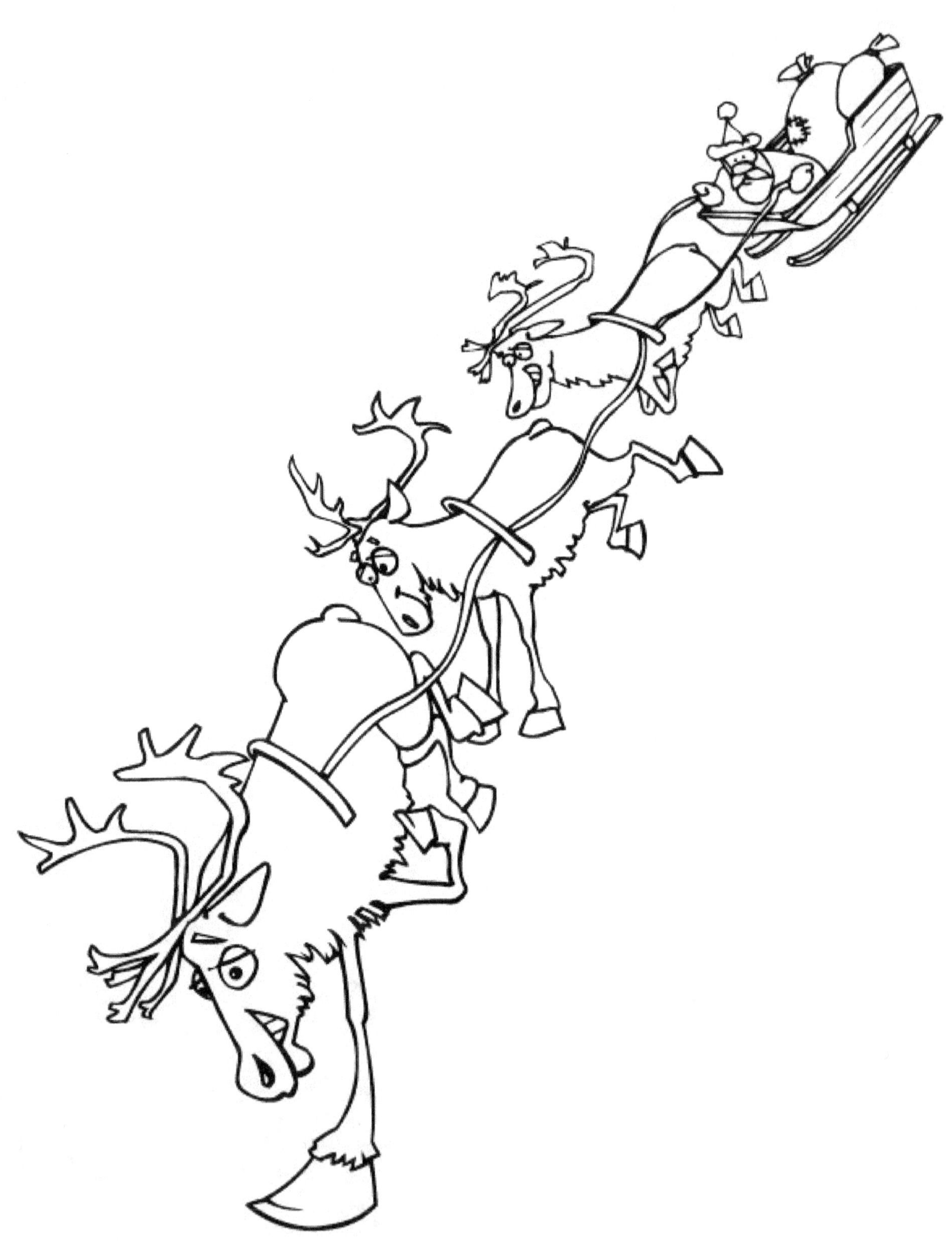

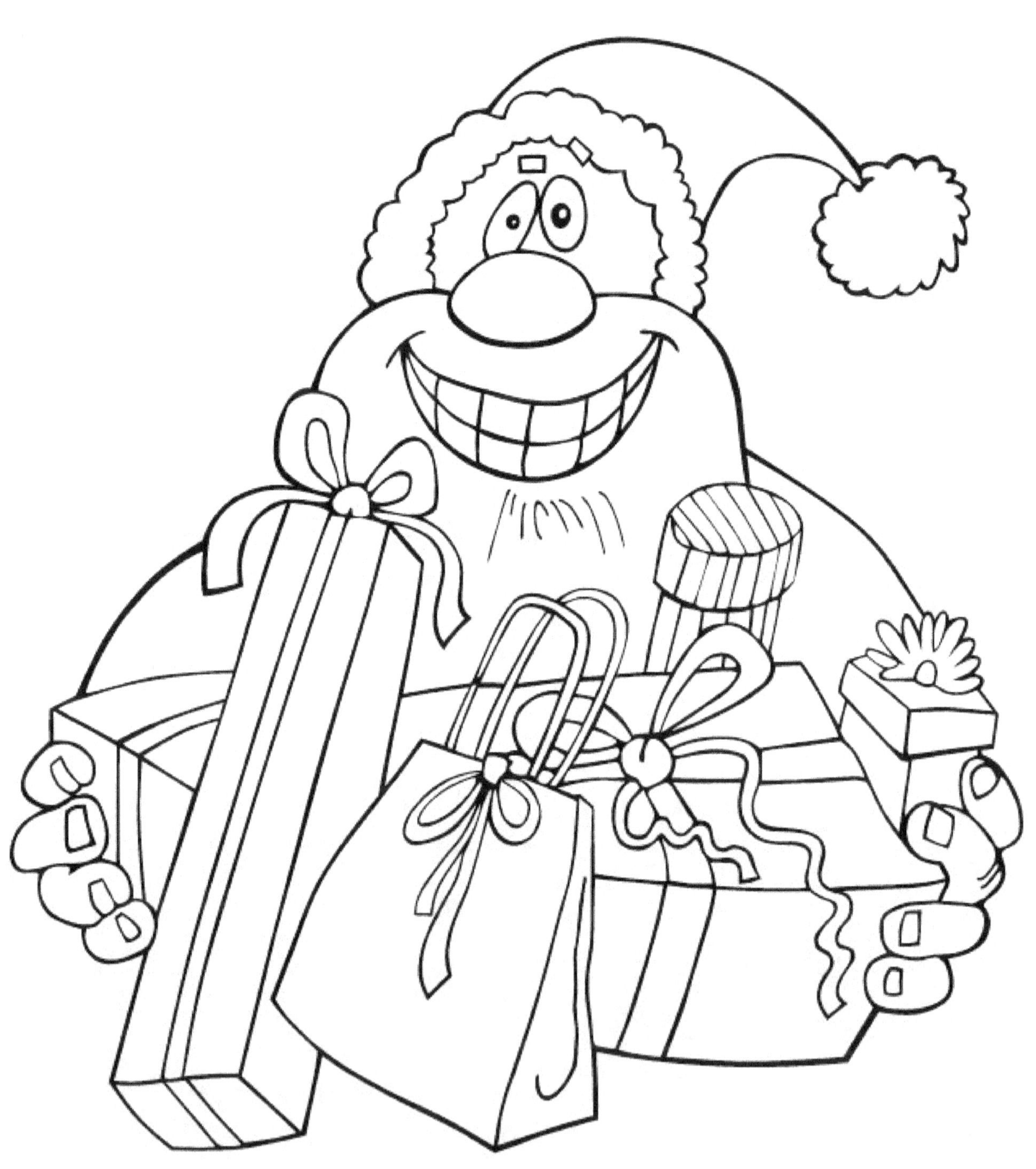

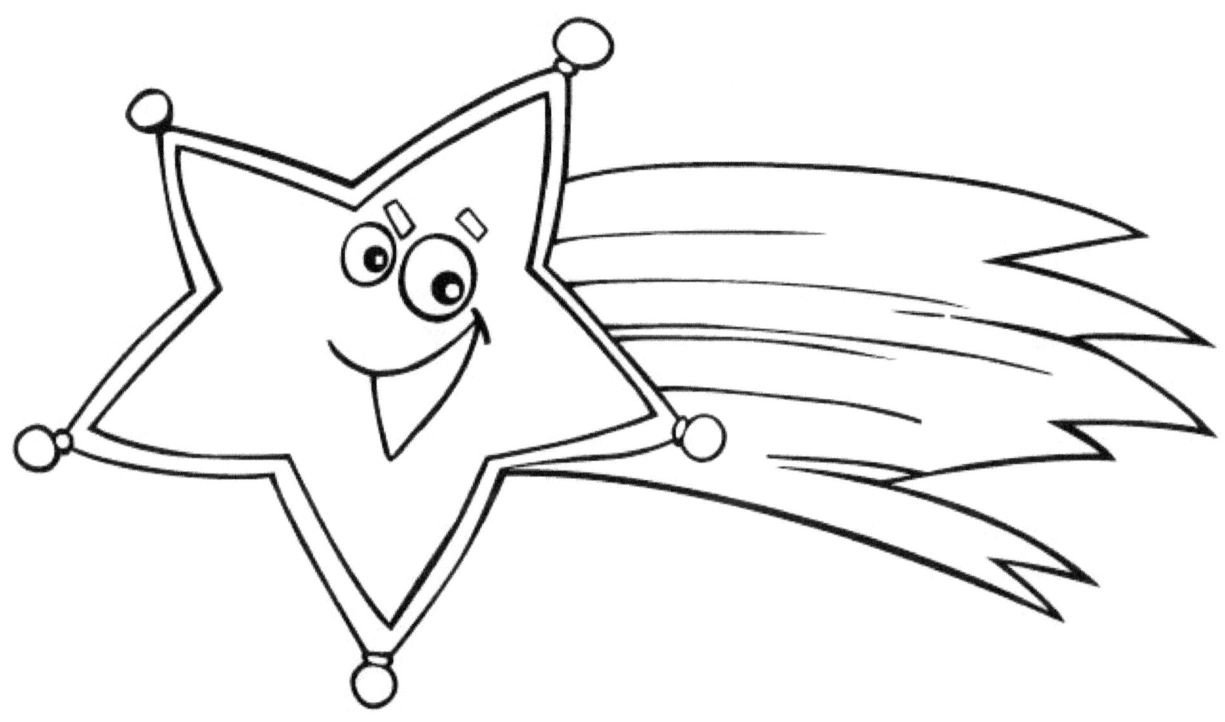

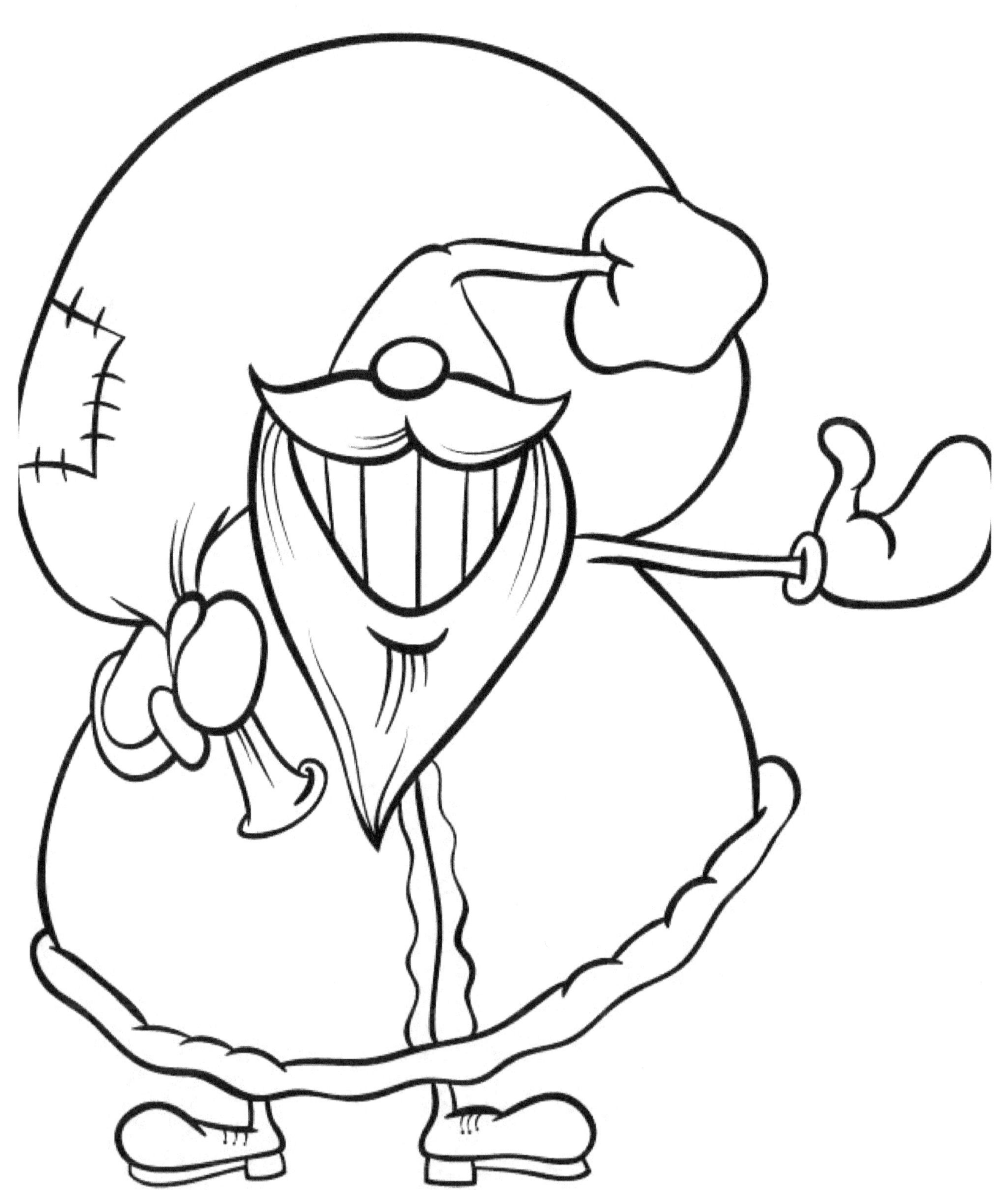

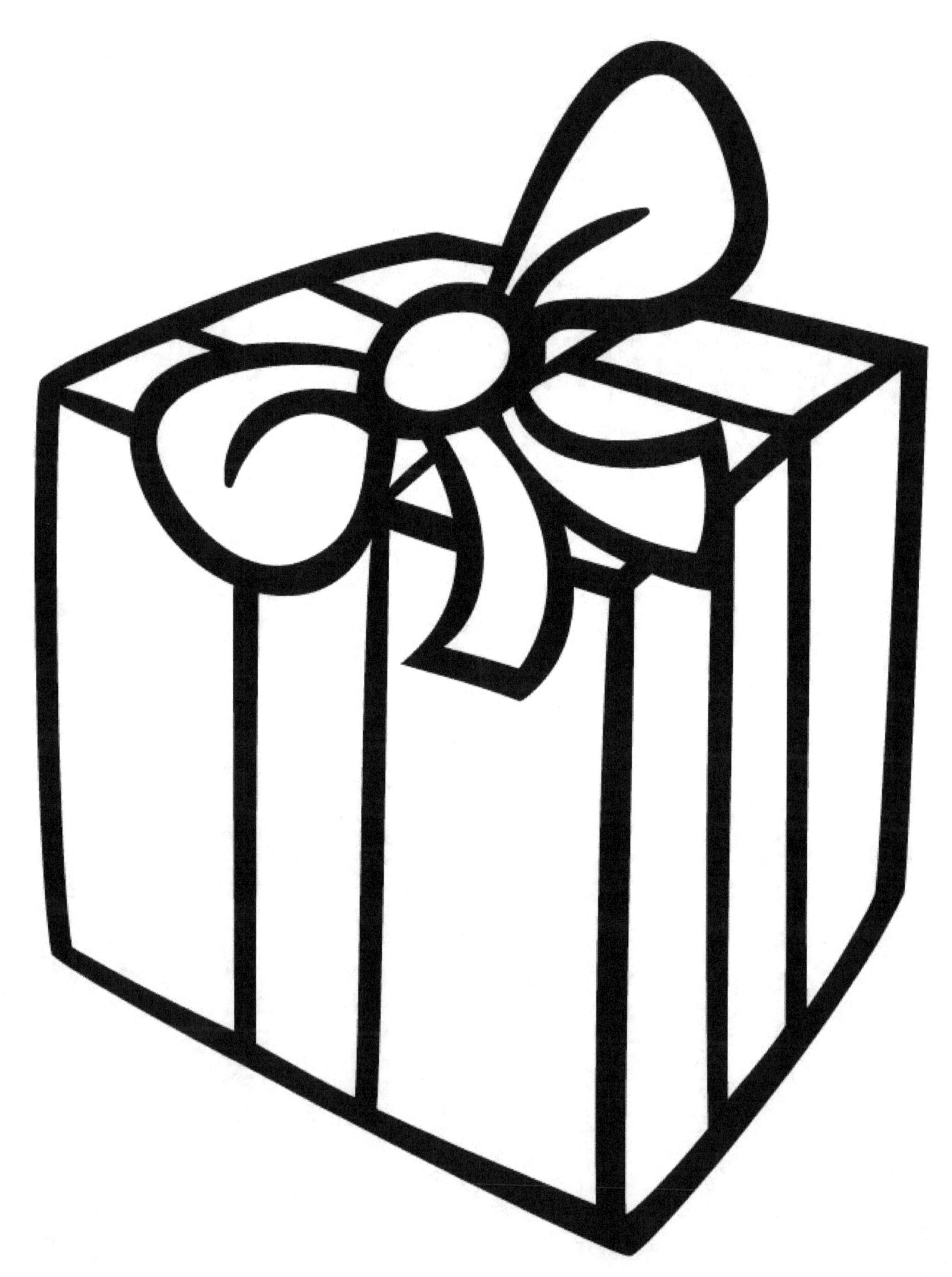

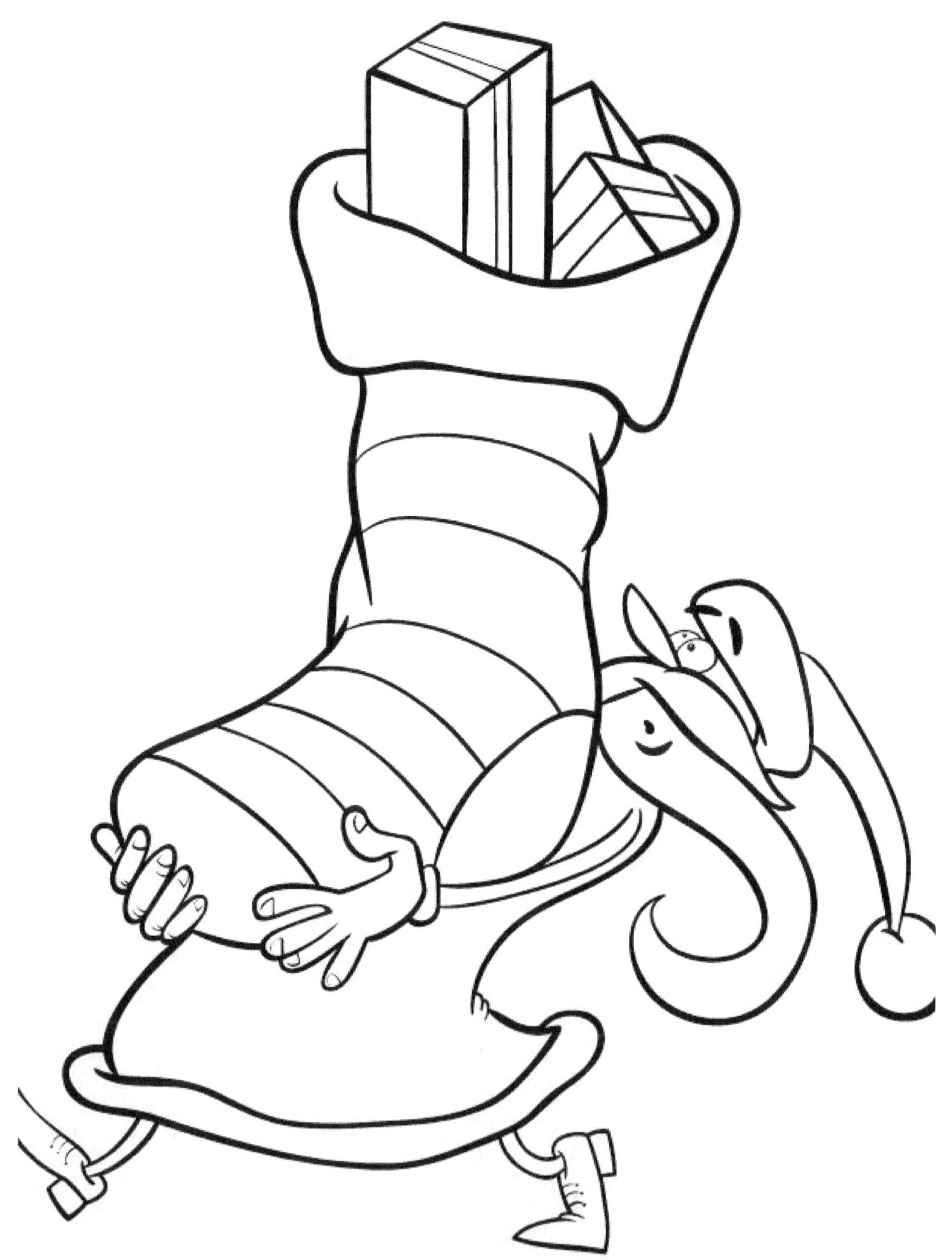

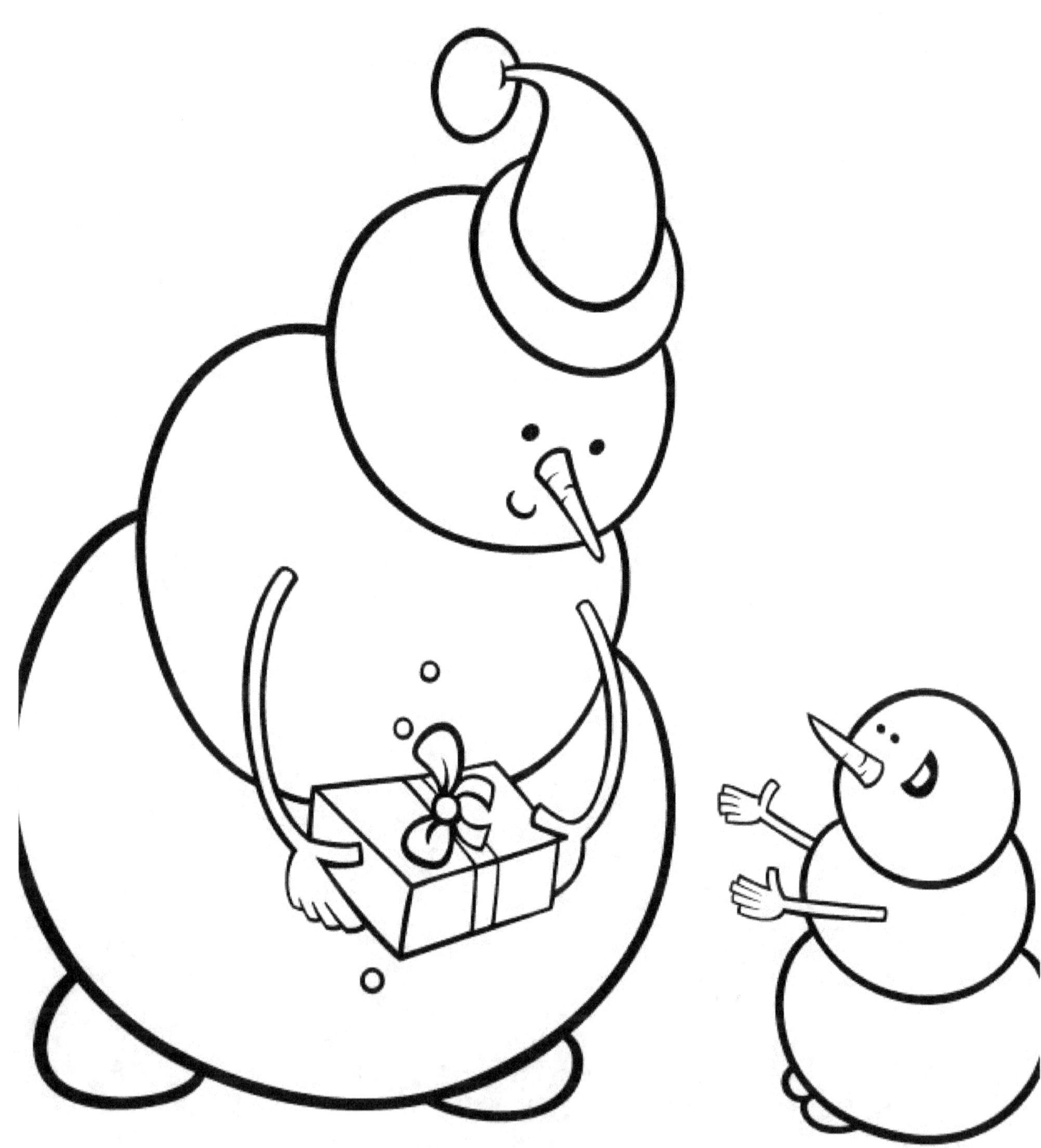

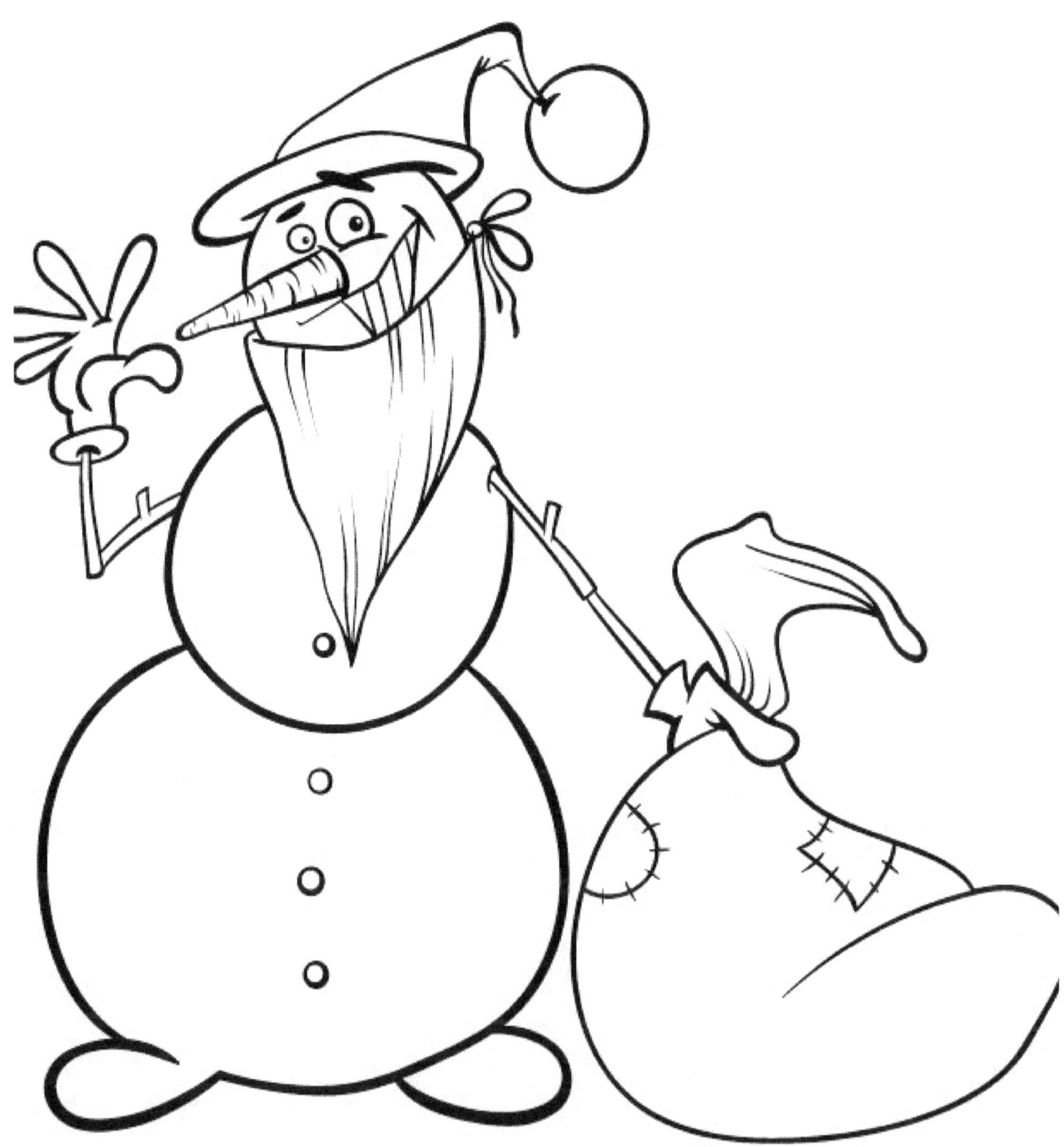

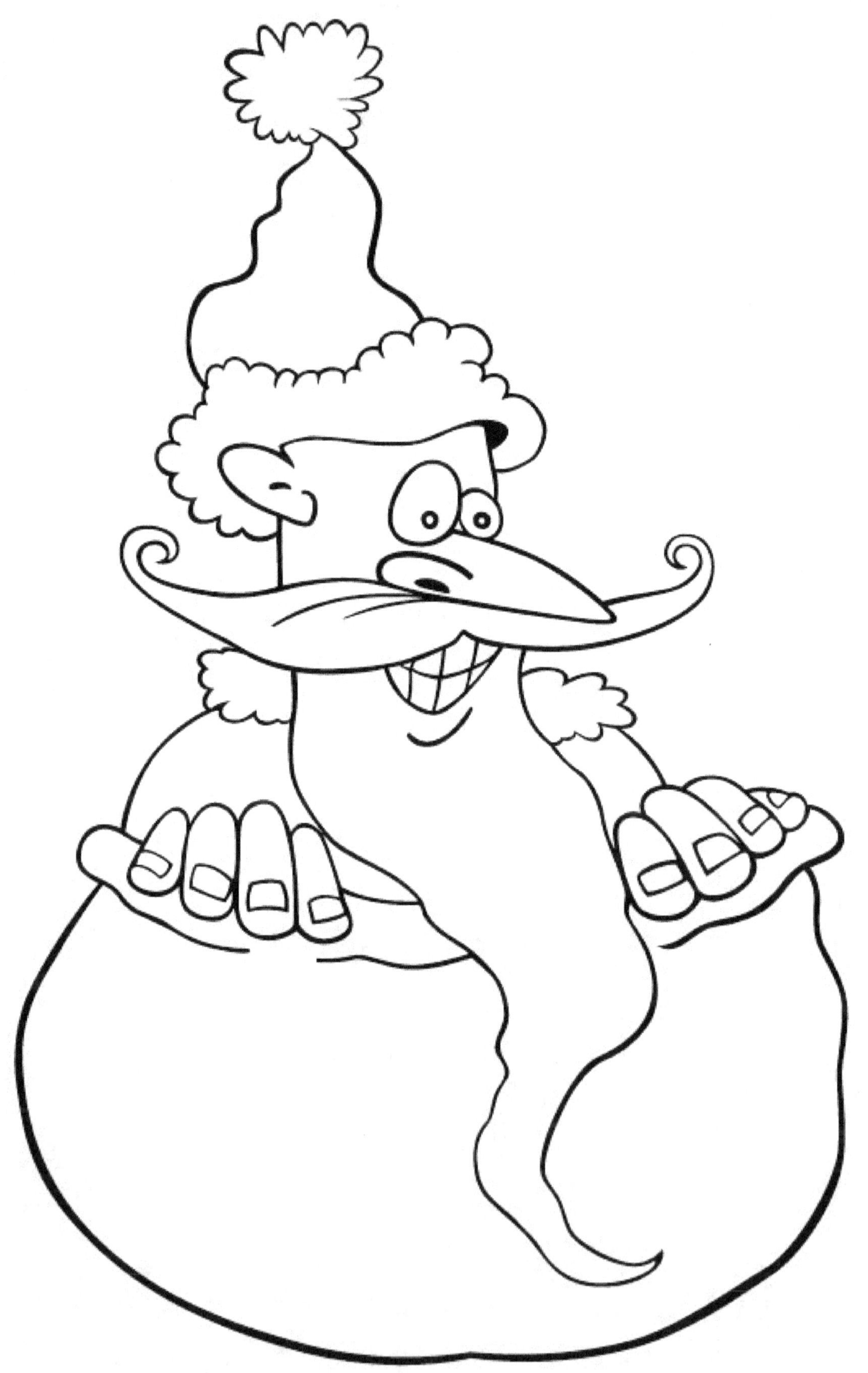

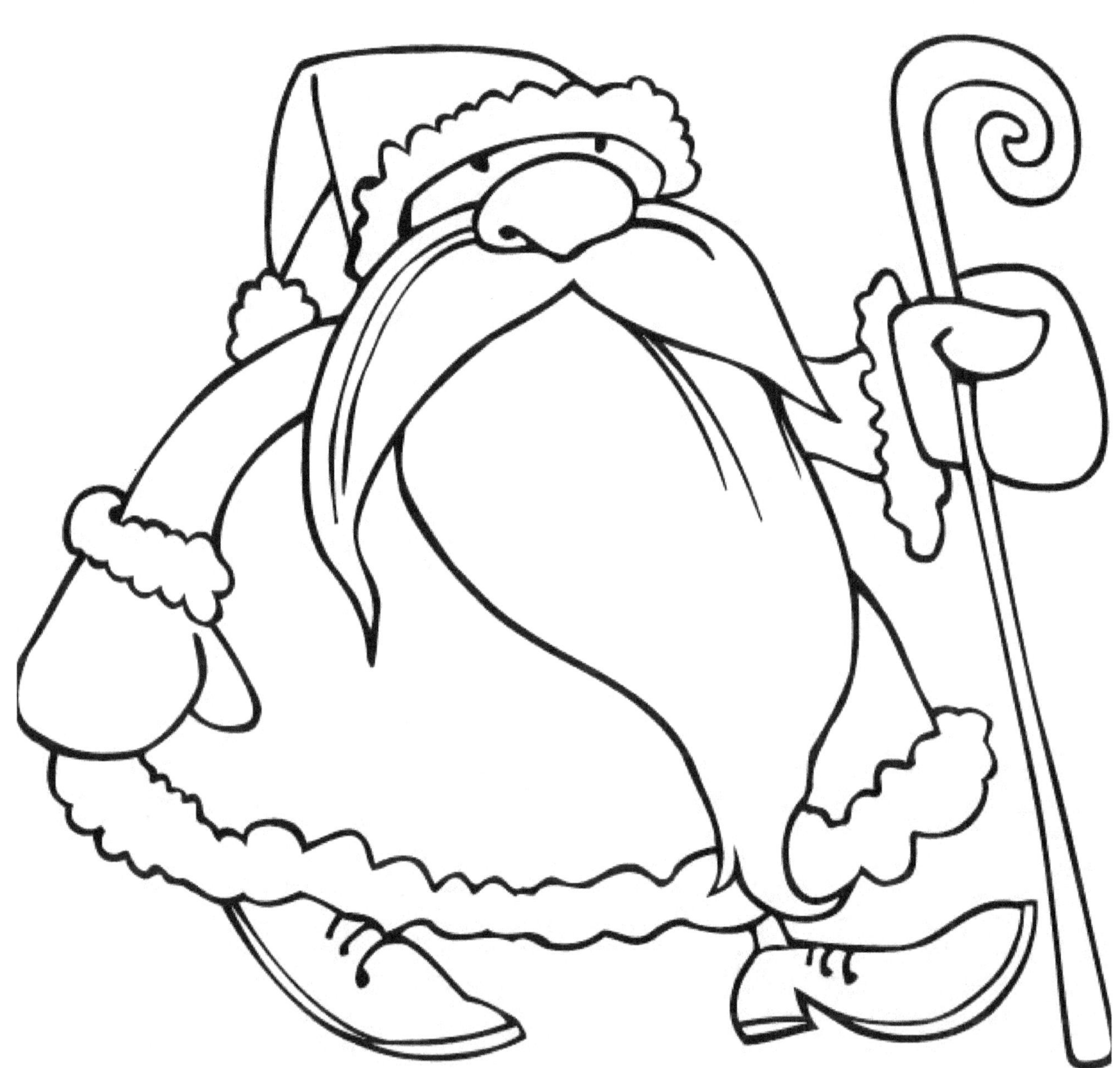

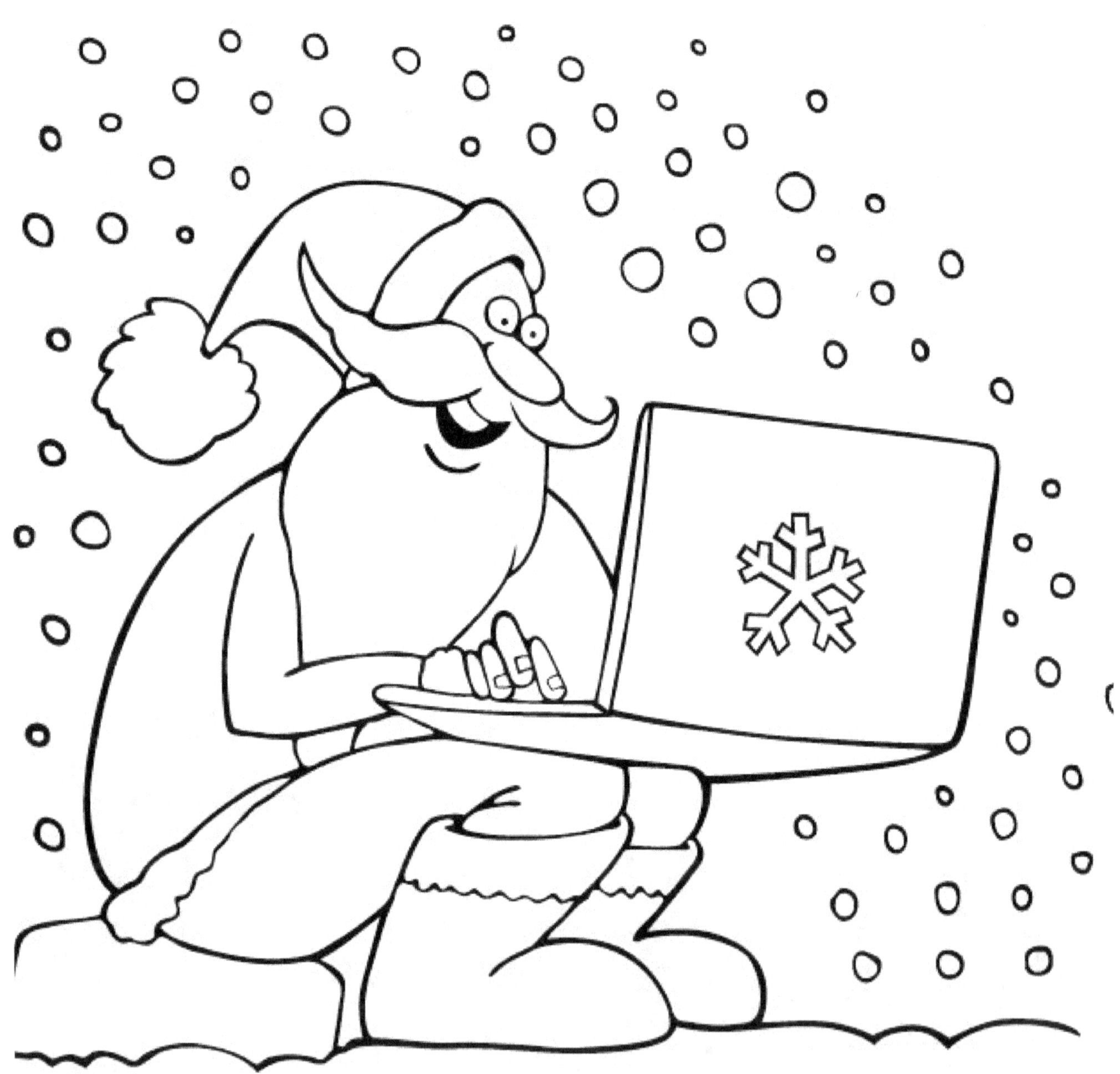

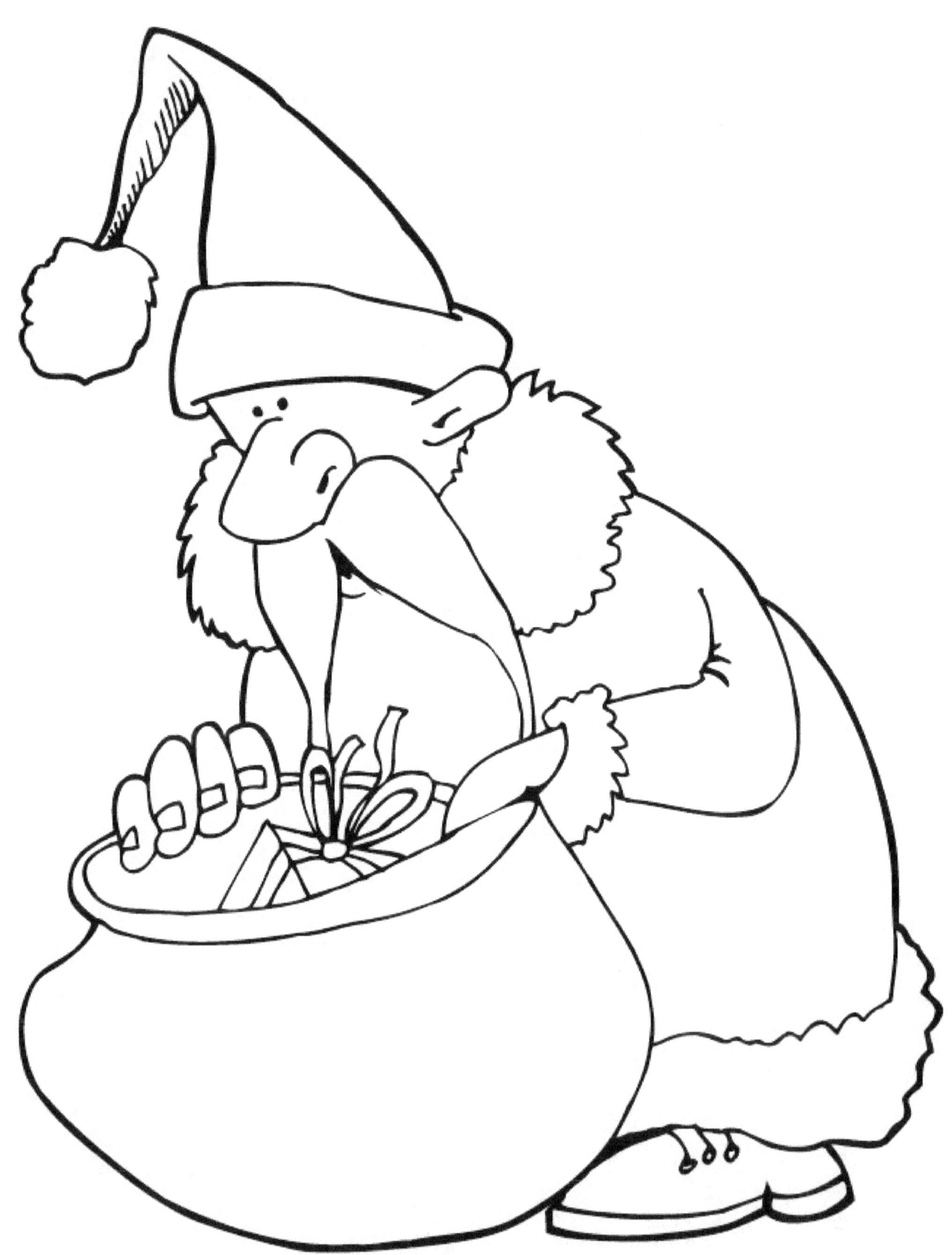

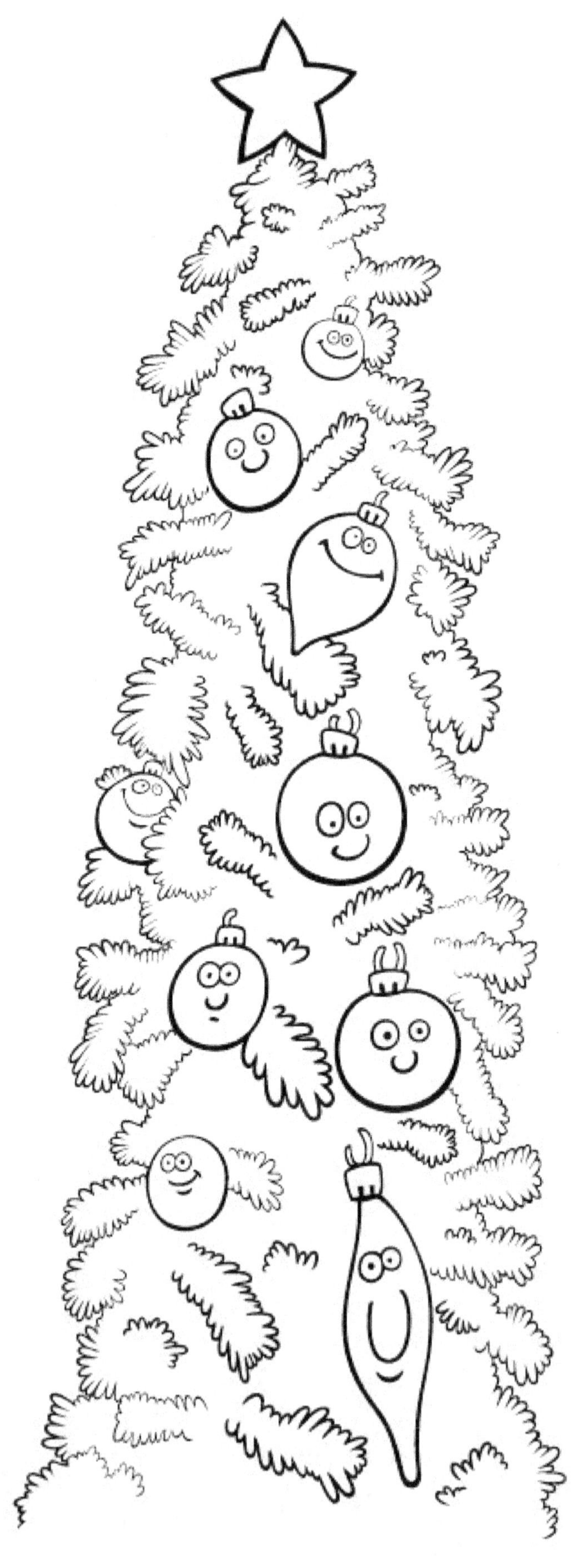

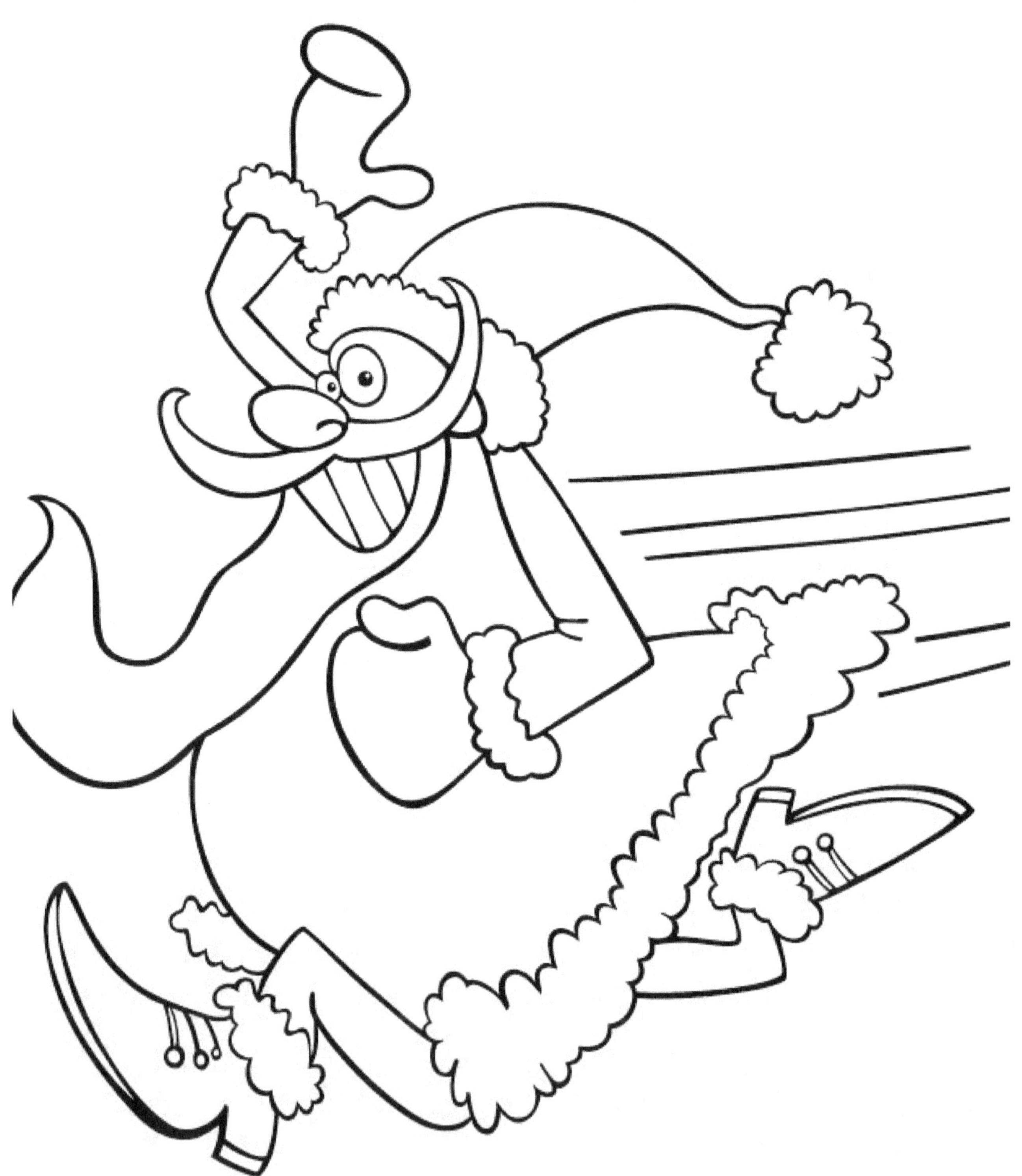

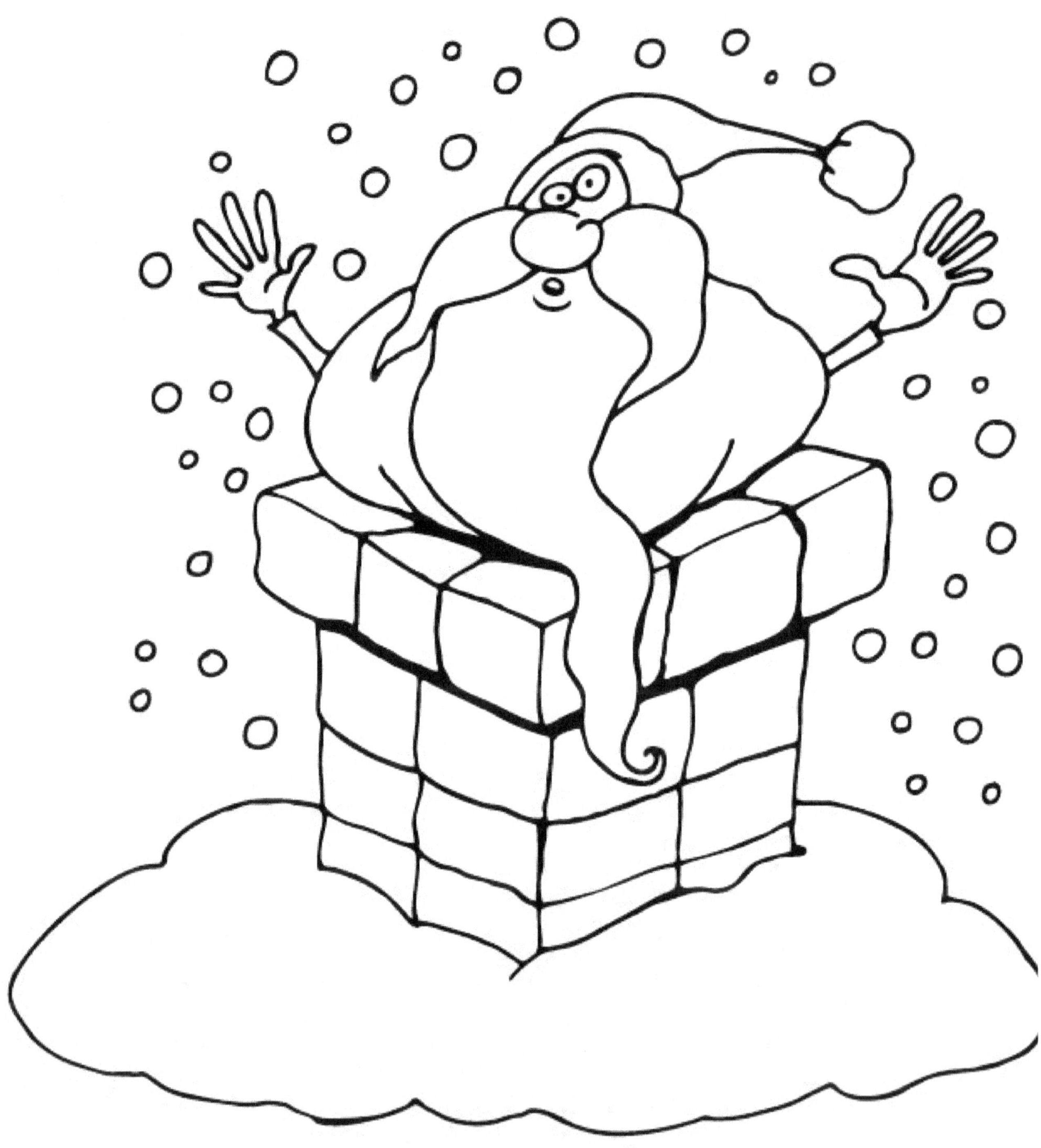

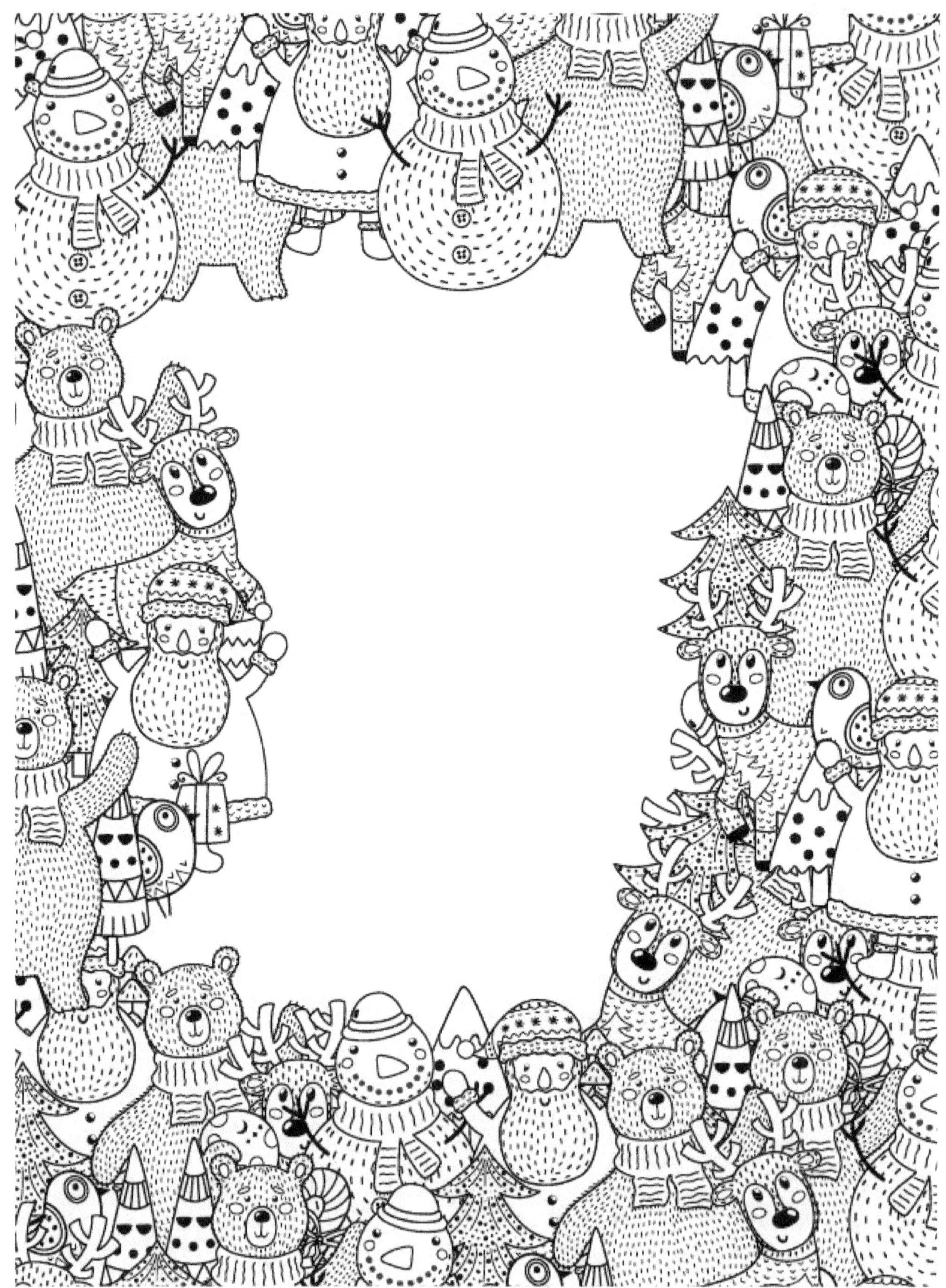

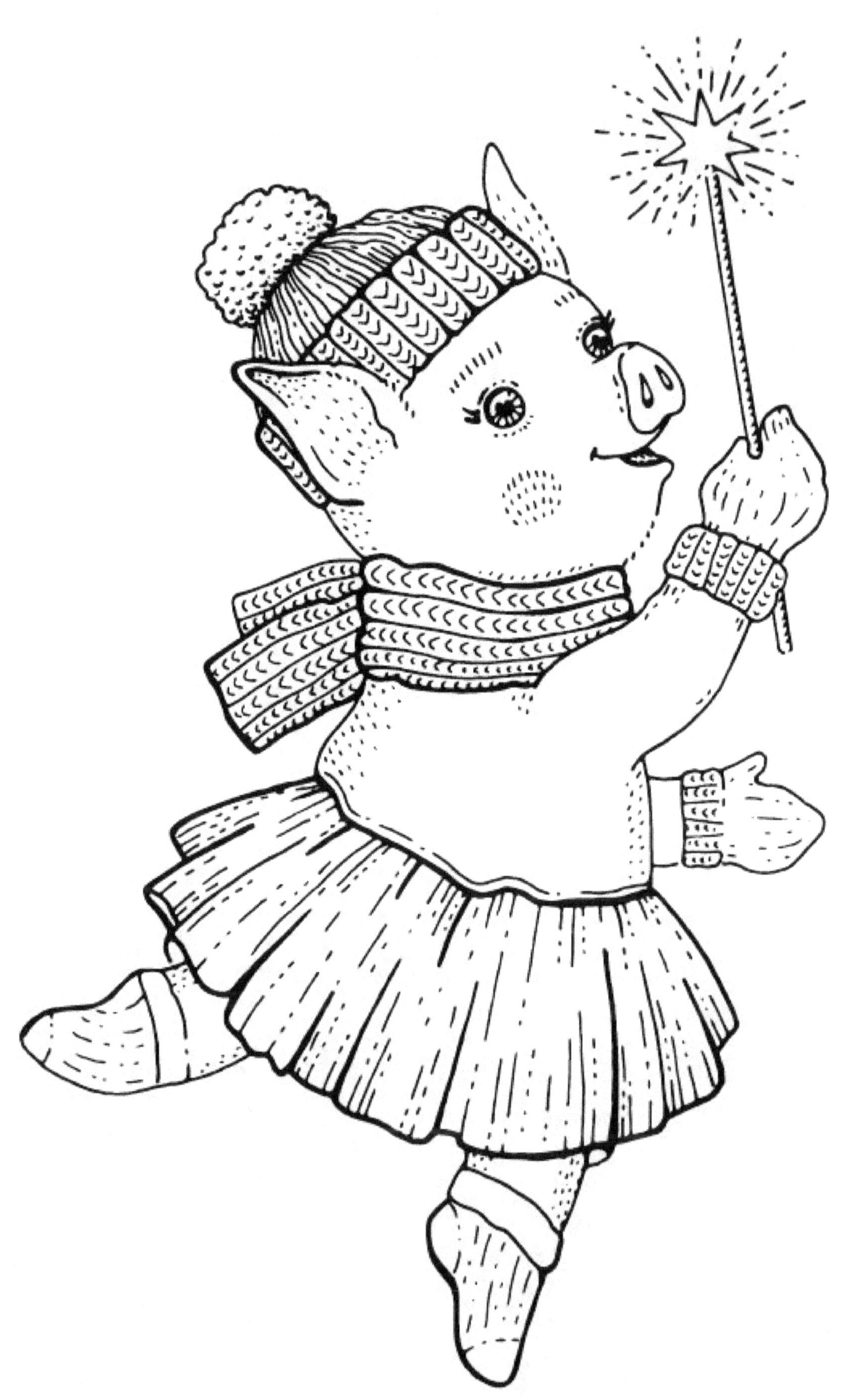

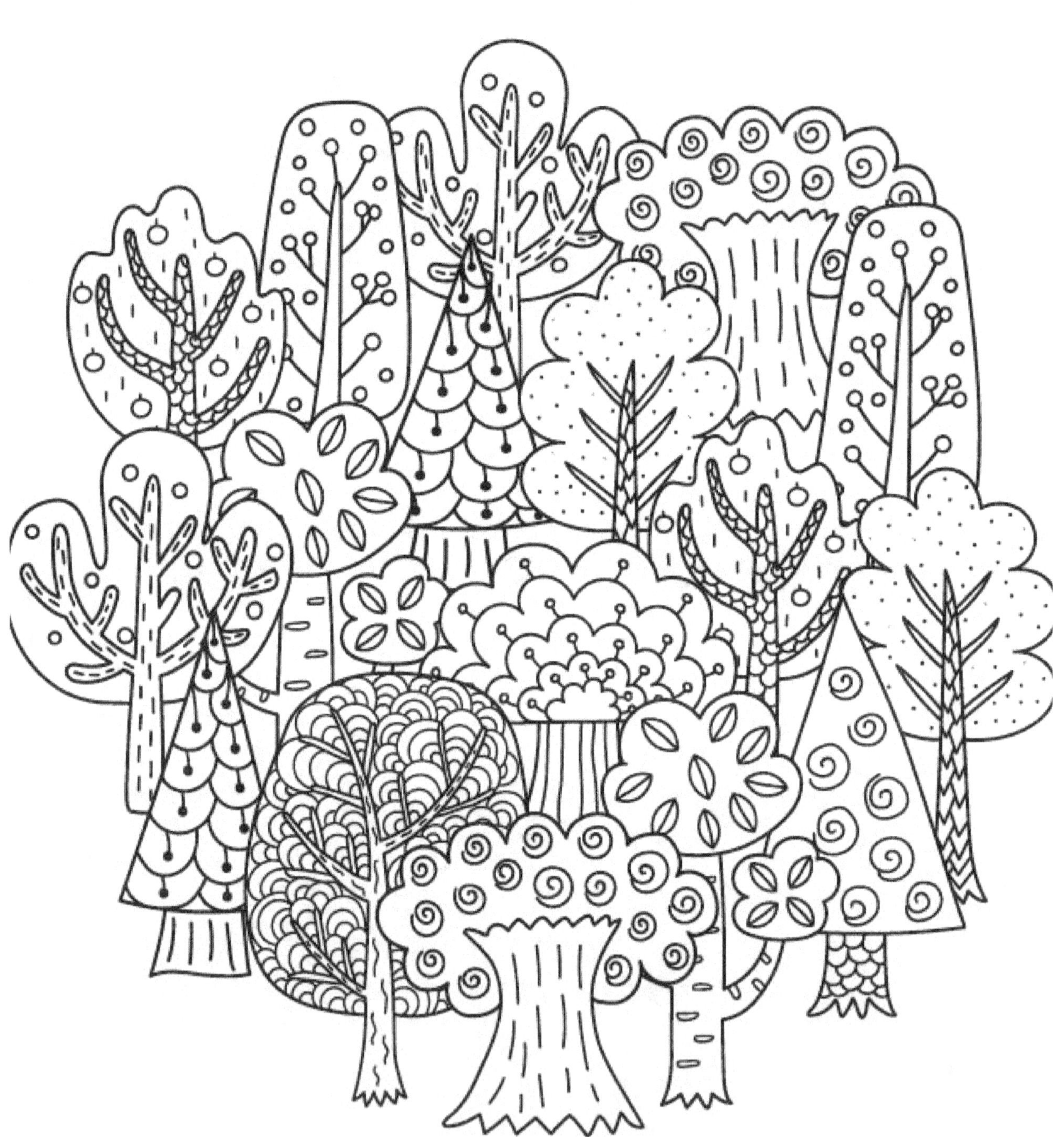

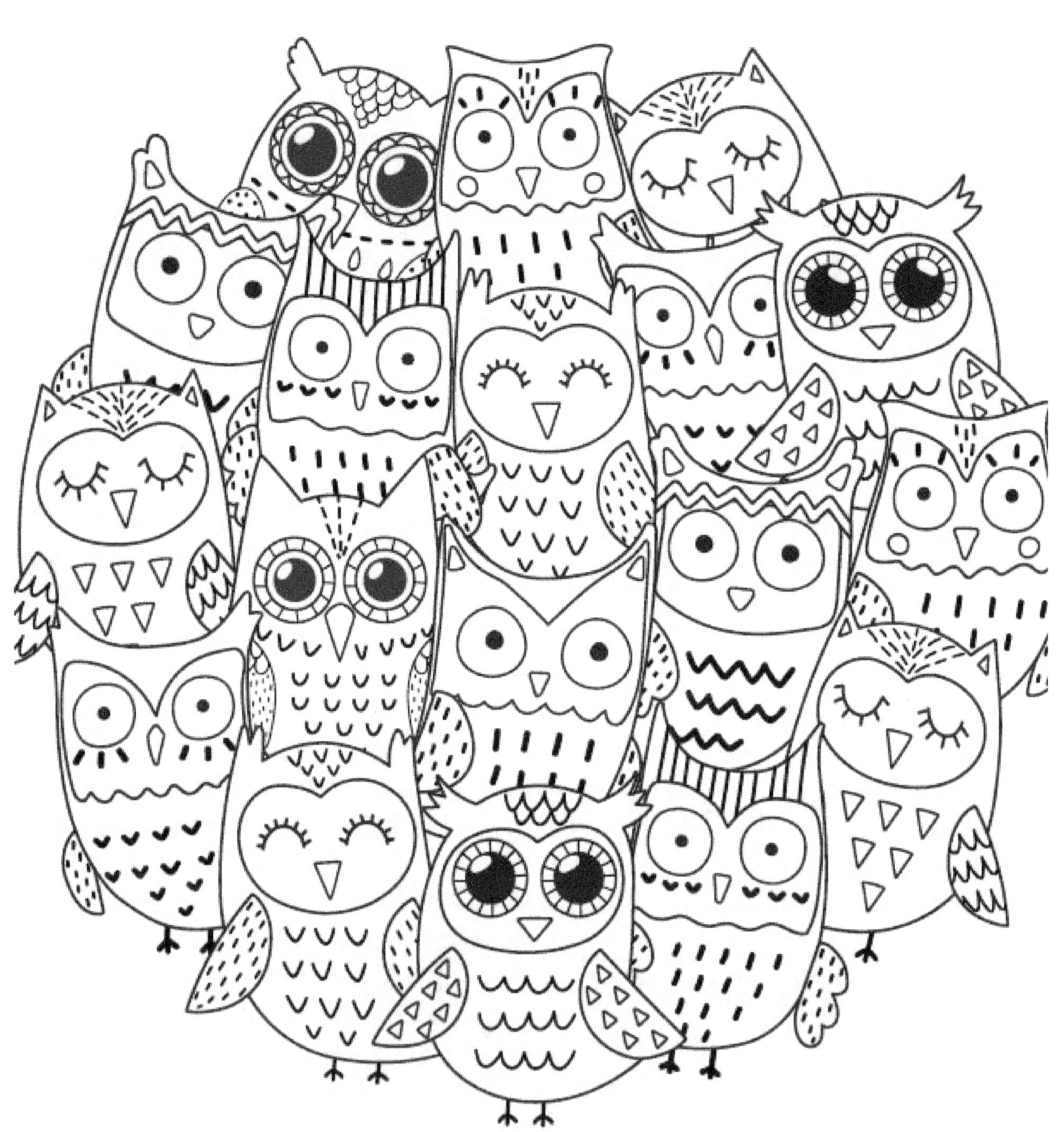

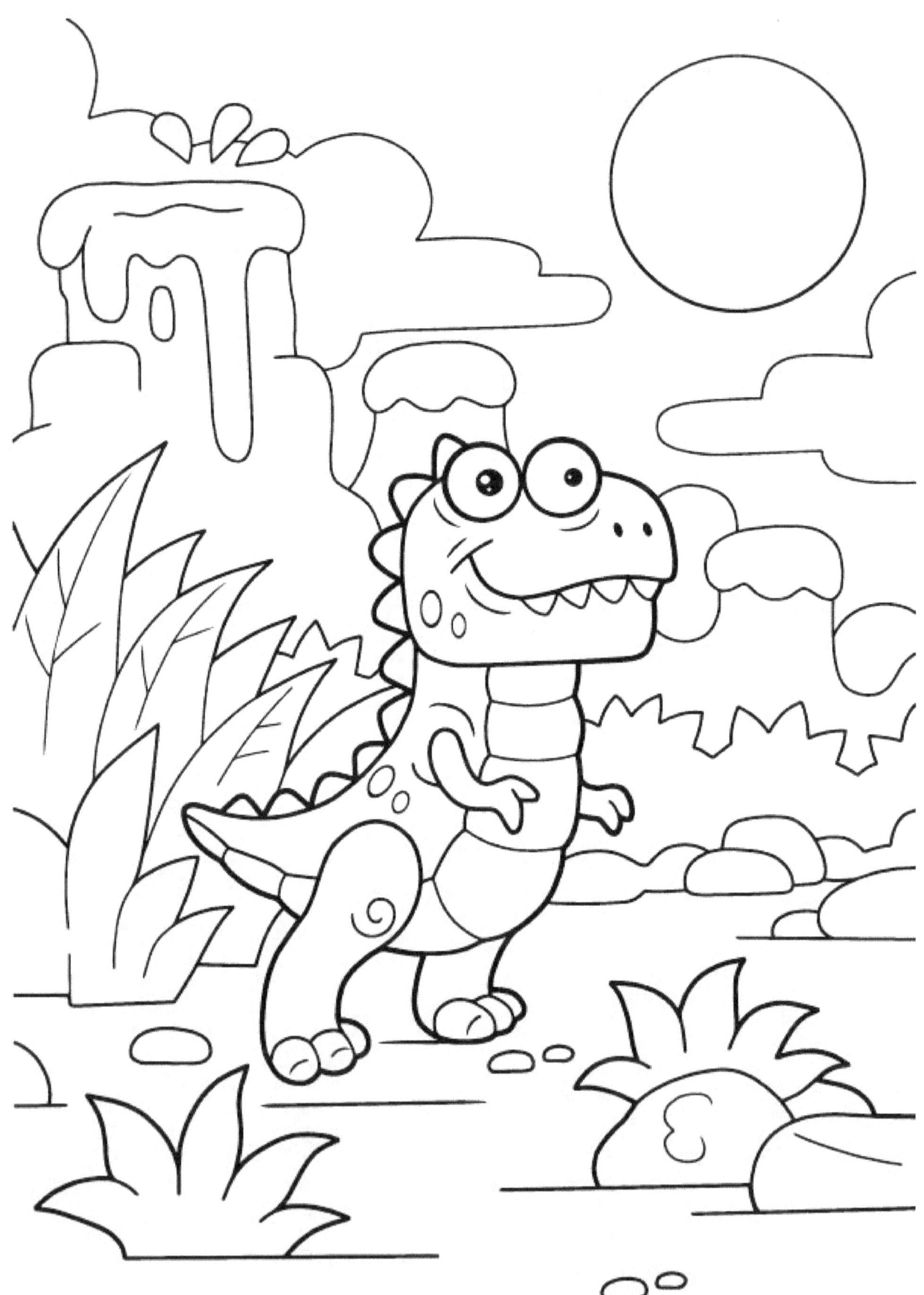

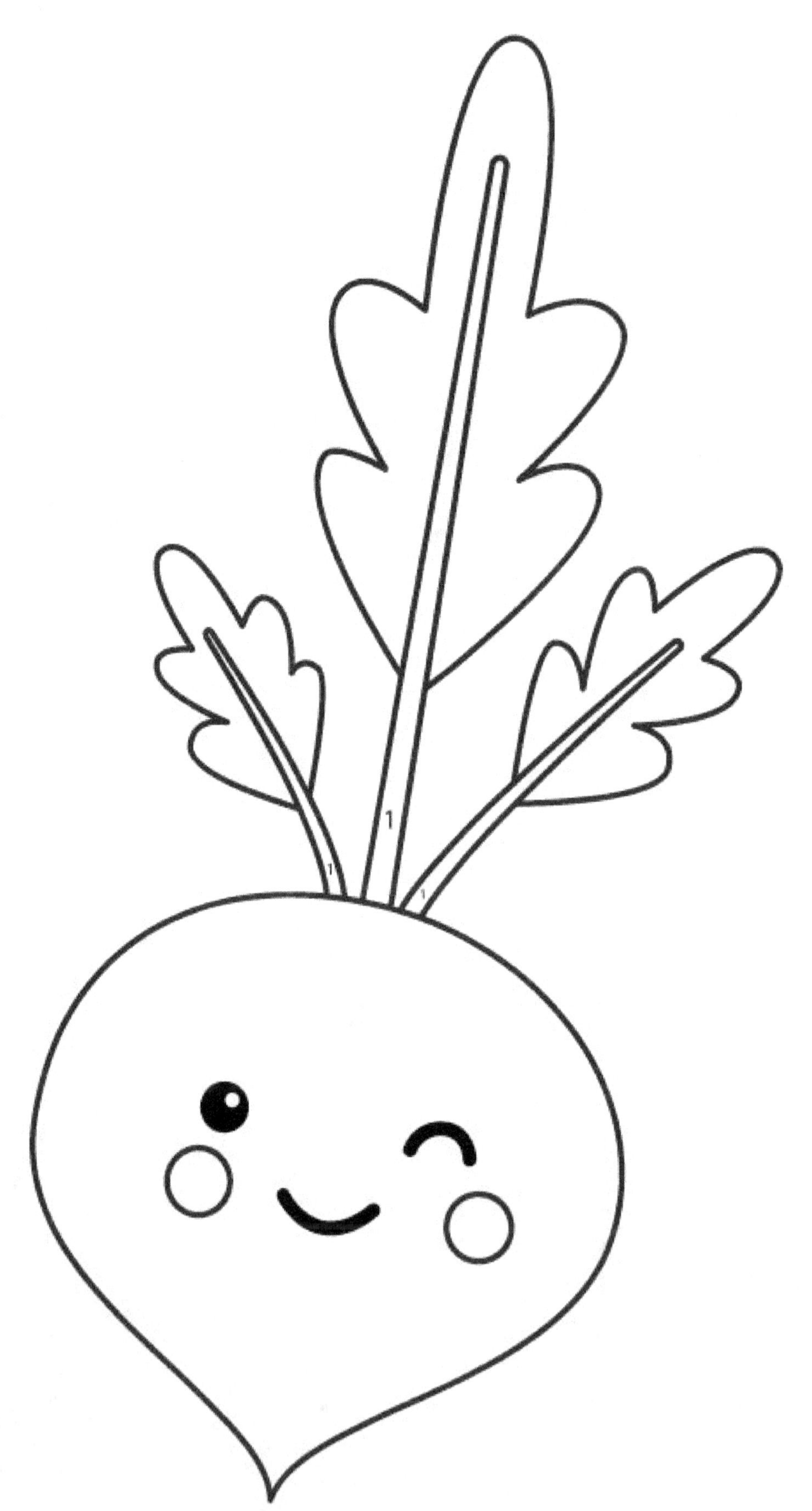

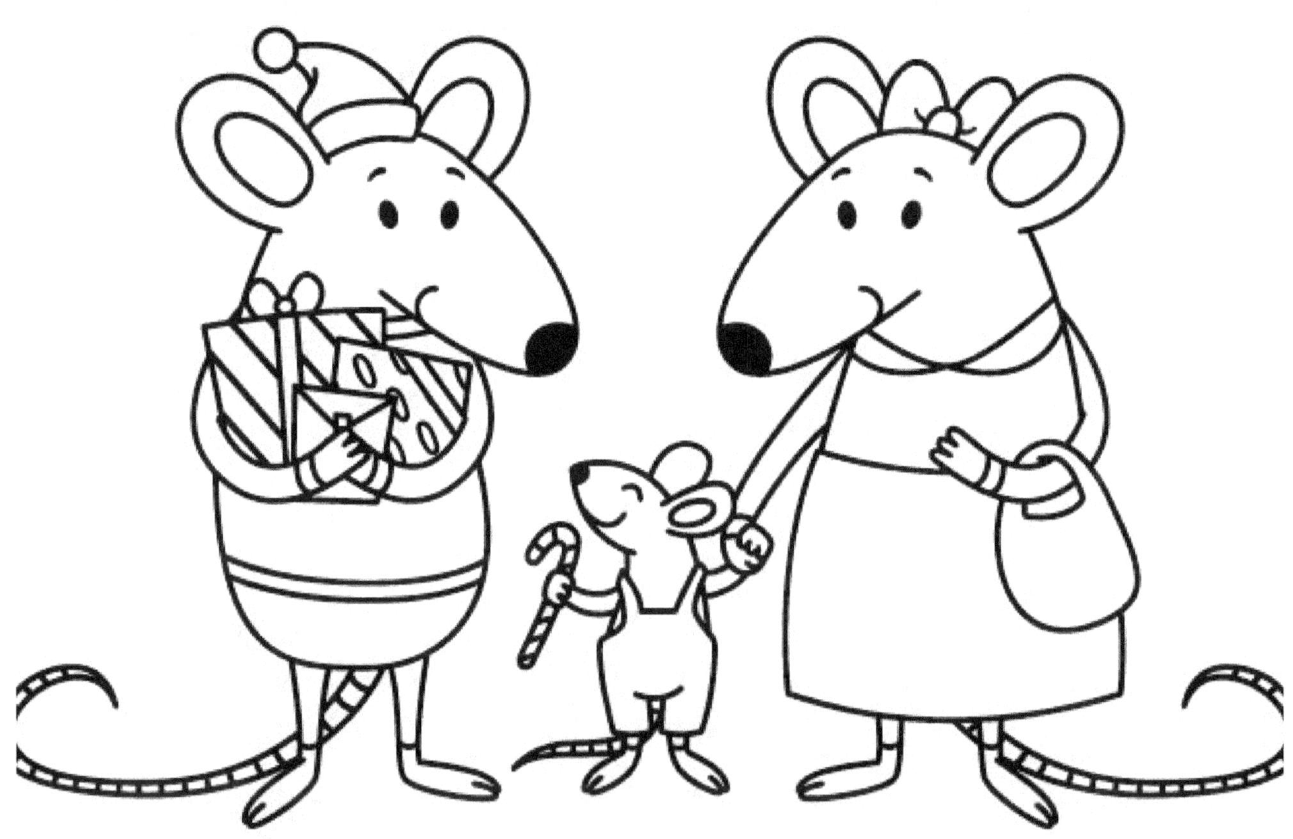

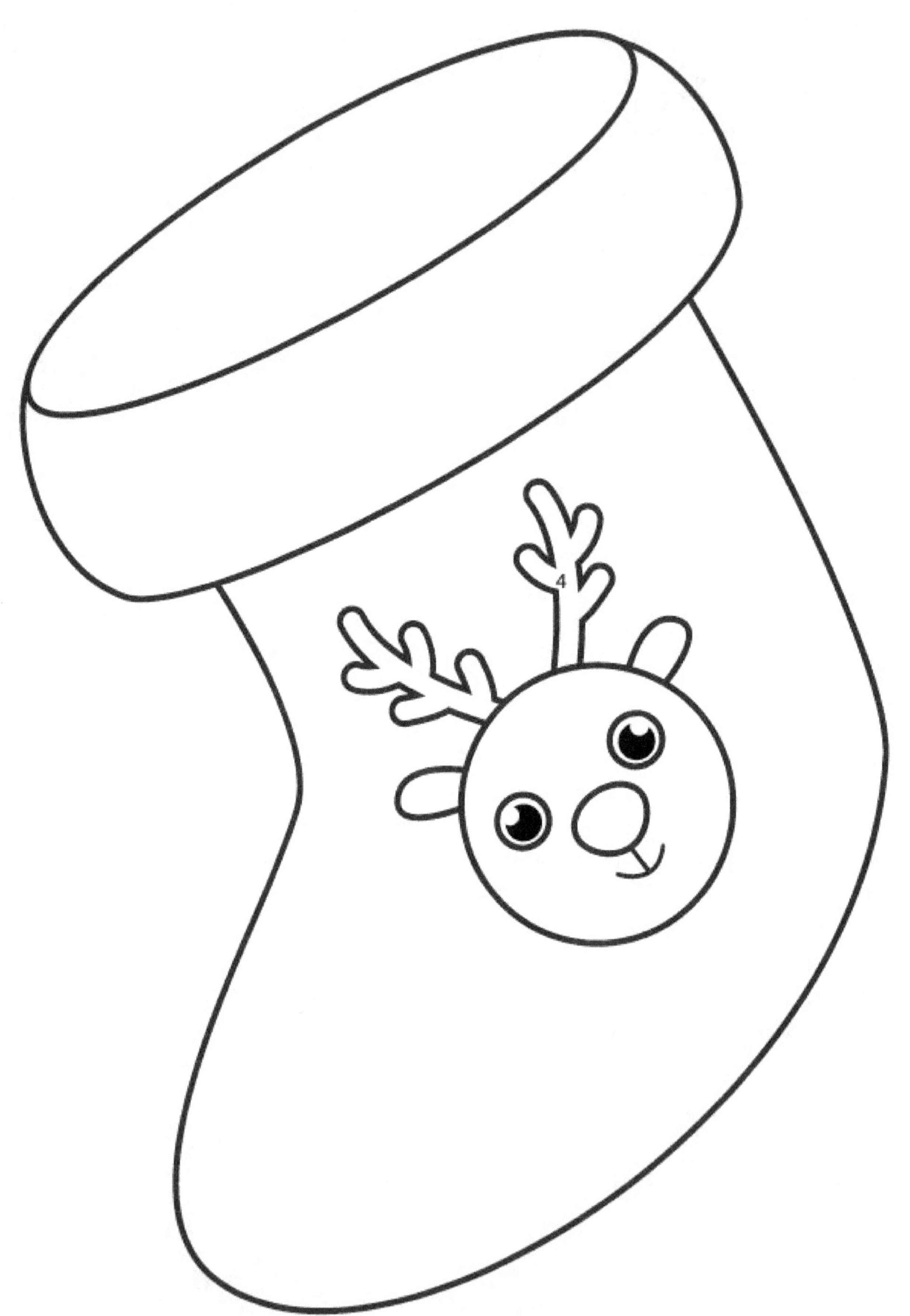

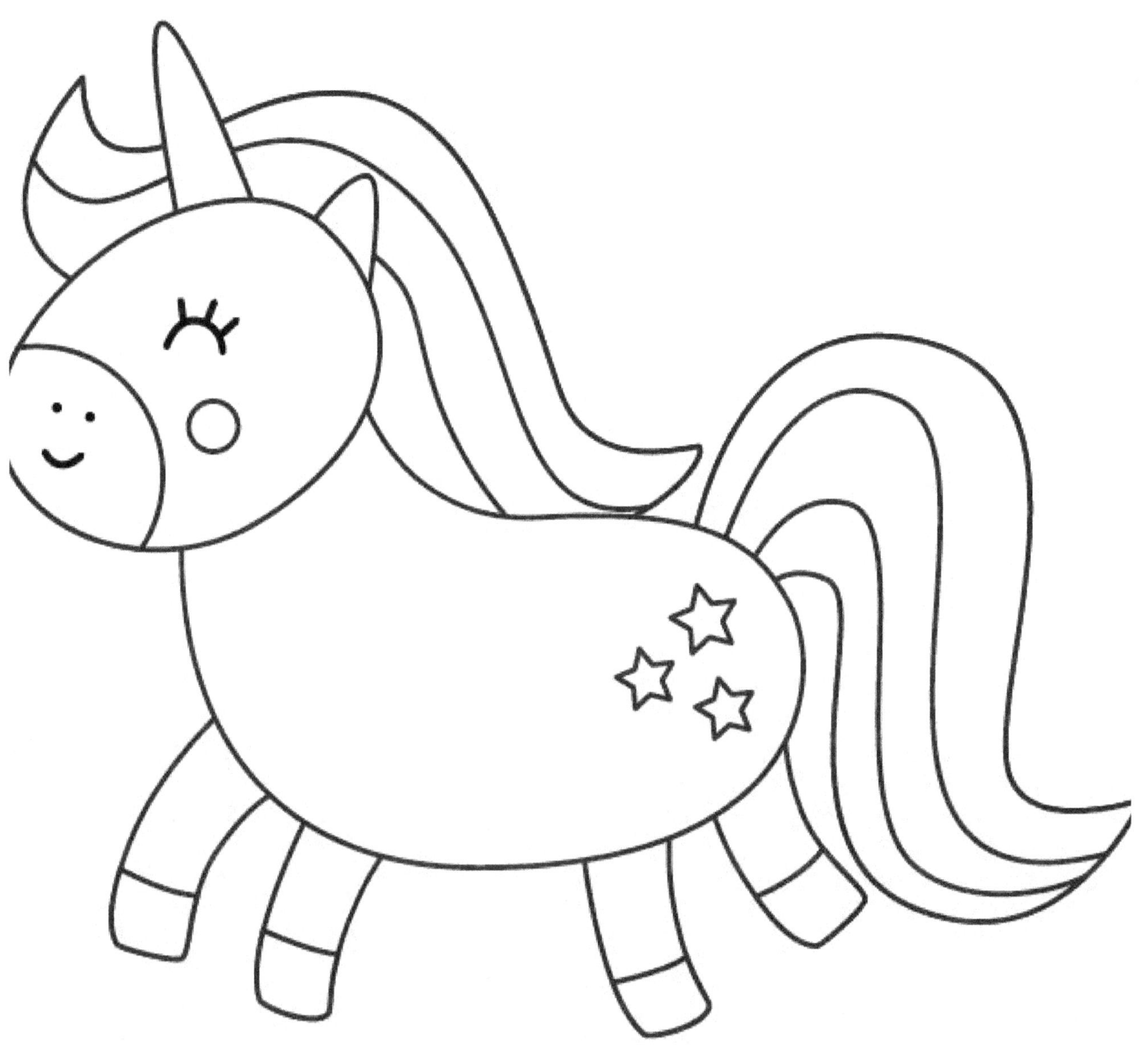

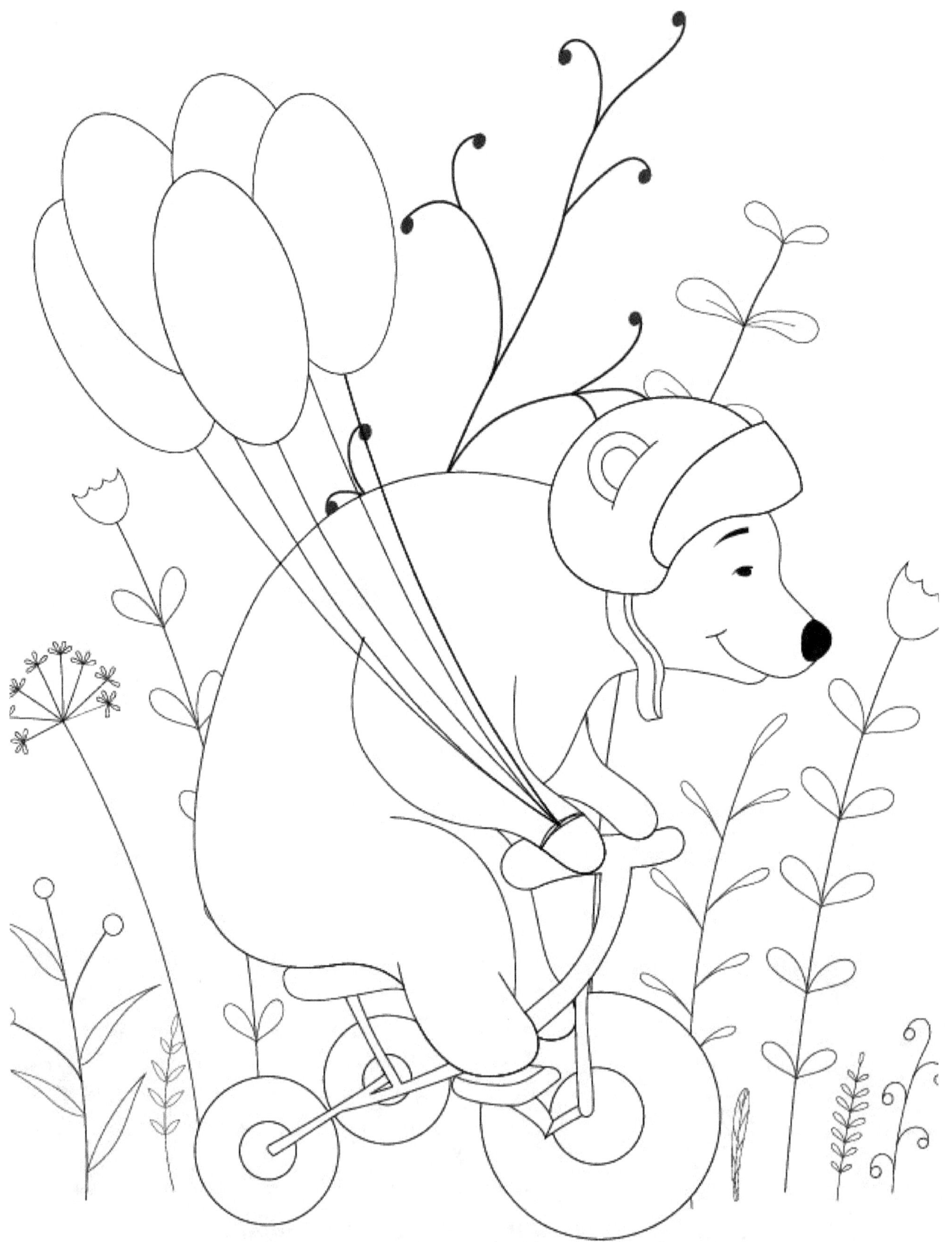